W9-BBM-059

DOROTHY LEE is the author of *Freedom and Culture* (Prentice-Hall) and a wide range of articles in philosophy, sociology, anthropology, education, and psychology.

A colleague of many years said this of her:
"she steeped herself in the lives of children and families,
bringing with her a unique human presence, sparkling humor,
vital dialogue, and determination to awaken
the full power of individuality within community and in schools."

VALUING
THE SELF

*What We Can Learn
from Other Cultures*

Dorothy Lee

PRENTICE-HALL, INC.,
Englewood Cliffs, New Jersey

Library of Congress Cataloging in Publication Data

LEE, DOROTHY D
    Valuing the self. *what we can learn from other cultures,*
    (A Spectrum Book) *Englewood Cliffs, Prentice-Hall,*
    Includes bibliographies. *Inc., 1976.*
    1. Culture and personality. 2. Socialization.
3. Self-realization. 4. Worth. I. Title.
GN504.L44   301.2′1   75-31996
ISBN 0-13-940114-8
ISBN 0-13-940106-7 pbk.

© 1976 by Prentice-Hall, Inc.
Englewood Cliffs, New Jersey

A SPECTRUM BOOK

COVER ILLUSTRATION, *Buffalo Hunt* by Alfred Miller, is used by permission of the Thomas Gilcrease Institute of American History and Art, Tulsa, Oklahoma.

Printed in the United States of America

10 9 8 7 6 5 4 3 2 1

Prentice-Hall International, Inc. *(London)*
Prentice-Hall of Australia Pty., Ltd. *(Sydney)*
Prentice-Hall of Canada, Ltd. *(Toronto)*
Prentice-Hall of India Private Limited *(New Delhi)*
Prentice-Hall of Japan, Inc. *(Tokyo)*
Prentice-Hall of Southeast Asia (Pte.) Ltd. *(Singapore)*

To Clark Moustakas
whose encouragement enabled this volume
to come to be

066142

CONTENTS

INTRODUCTION

The primary focus of this collection of essays is autonomy and community as these relate to the individual self and recognize, affirm, and encourage the growth of the self. By *community* I mean the people around me—my parents, my teachers, my friends, even a passerby who looks at me or nudges me. By *autonomy* I mean being in charge of myself. I mean that I see with my own eyes, not what I am told is there. I mean that I relate to the world with inquiry, *my* inquiry. When I look at the tree, I am not even limited by the expectation of my own self. I look at it freshly, alertly; I become involved in the miracle, I create it out of my own perception. It does not occur to me to question my perception. I trust it. *I* decide if I like it or not, *I* am filled with joy or concern or disgust. In all my being, when I feel, when a thought buds and develops, I greet my feeling and my thinking. I am myself.

However, when children come home filled with the desire to share their adventures; when they bring forth new ideas and no one listens; when what they say is dismissed as unimportant; when they are not recognized and are told that they are wrong: the tree is really ugly, the robin's song is really grating; when community does not value the self, children come to regard their own senses and thoughts as worthless, and they substitute instead what they are supposed to think and feel.

Community, however, can also recognize and honor. The mother can listen with excitement to what her child tells her, asking questions, transacting. The child responds and suddenly realizes that he or she has not looked carefully enough, has not thought hard enough. Creative perception, original thinking are tremendously demanding. It is so much easier, for instance, to read a review of Kafka first so as to "know" what he says, or to "know" whether the book is good. It is so much easier to see "a" tree rather than "this" tree. So community has a further function. It evokes. It shakes the individual into greater effort. It does this because it honors the autonomy of the individual.

Some years ago, I published a book of selections of my articles. I had written them for my colleagues as a form of communication. When they appeared as a book, they were used in undergraduate courses. And I found out, with horror and guilt, that the students I talked to had found *the* truth. I was the author, I gave the authoritative statement. I could not even argue with them because they answered me back from the authority of my book. I felt that I had dumped a load of gravel on new, thin, weak, gloriously alive grass, or even on seed that had never had a chance to sprout. I had killed. I vowed that I would never publish a collection of papers again.

I no longer wrote with joy and anticipation. My writing became a withdrawal from life; I had to withdraw from the world around me—from people, birds, houses, clouds, trucks, everything —in order to concentrate on some abstract idea or respond to questions that were no longer alive in me. I had to struggle to bring myself to the point of writing. Finally, I refused to write. When invited to a conference, I simply lectured. I had a carefully worked out outline; I arrived with my notes all carefully arranged so that my C followed my B logically and my B followed my A logically; but they were always *my* C following *my* B and there was no room for community to affect what I was saying; there was no crack through which community could enter. Eventually, I gave a talk without notes and it was then that I realized what I was really moving toward: I was trying to reach the point where I could help people whose thinking and sensing had not been honored and had been substituted by the "correct" ideas and perceptions of their teachers and textbooks. I stopped writing or lecturing. I started forming graduate seminars, usually with young adults and middle-aged students. I could not wait to hear what the students said. If I waited it was because the other members of the seminar, recognizing a valid idea, were full of their own responses. I listened not patiently until they were through, but impatiently, because I was entranced watching the weak, little blades of grass begin to grow in stature and strength. The students forgot to feel shame in case they were saying something silly or presenting unacceptable, "wrong" views or asking foolish questions. They wrote me papers full of their own thinking and feeling, with immense margins so that I would not simply "correct" their papers but discuss with them as an equal. They learned to value their own fleeting responses. It did not take long for the whole seminar to learn to listen with interest and participate with involvement. Nothing was dead. The struggling sprouts had not been killed; they only needed to be greeted.

I held to my decision not to publish another collection for years. (Parenthetically, I cannot imagine life without reading and am grateful to the writers I like.) But gradually I realized that for many I was really offering and opening alternatives, not laying down dogma.

This last year, I received many letters from former students, academic colleagues, and others, for whom something I said furnished a crack for a new idea or helped stretch out the vision of an old one. At that point, I decided to publish this small selection.

In the chapters that follow I have chosen to explore ideas that recognize community and autonomy as basic to the emergence and development of the creativity and health of the individual. I am concerned with distinguishing between value as residing in a situation, as inherent in reality, in contrast to values that are the basis for making judgments, for determining right or wrong. I want also to show that where the individual is fully engaged in life that motivations are autonomous, that the person is invited to act, moving, thrusting forward, striving, aspiring, rather than being motivated by needs, drives, and tensions. The behavior of the autonomous individual is prodigal, exuberant, unpredictable in its reach.

In this book, I am also questioning the heavy price we pay for literacy, the damage to wonder, curiosity, questing, and sense of mystery. I am pointing to the destructive consequences of formalized conventional education when it robs the individual of unique, unpredictable experience and offers mainly authoritative statements, facts, and labels. I am concerned with the cultural factors that inhibit or encourage the development of the potential to learn—whether through society, family and community, or through the school, whatever it is that incites individuals to develop their potentials to the utmost, or what interferes and robs learners of the expression of this potential.

Another important focus of *Valuing the Self* is the relationship between freedom and structure, what I regard as the essential conditions of freedom, what I mean by freedom itself, and how "social constraint" frees me from the interference of others and makes it possible for me to act.

Throughout this book, when I speak of other societies the people I know best are the Sioux, whose education and life I know in great detail. I refer to them often to illustrate the way in which autonomy and community work together in creating individuals who value the self, individuals who speak to the powers within and reach out to life with new energy and vision.

CULTURE AND THE EXPERIENCE OF VALUE

I am concerned with the relation of human values to value itself. By human values, by *a* value or a system of values, I mean the basis upon which an individual chooses one course rather than another, judges as better or worse, right or wrong. We can speak about human values, but we cannot know them directly. We infer them through their expression in behavior.

What I refer to as value—not *a* value—resides in the situation, in the field in which an individual participates. What I call *a* value is cultural; what I call *value* resides in the reality which is mediated by culture. We experience value when our activity is permeated with satisfaction, when we find meaning in our life, when we feel good, when we act not out of calculating choice and not for extraneous purpose, but rather because this is the only way that we, as ourselves, deeply want to act. What I call value can be experienced only when there is uninterrupted relatedness, when the self is open to the experience of the other, of the surround; when, to use Dewey's term, it is transacting, not interacting. When the *other* in the transaction is human, value is social, though it is experienced by the individual self. In this sense, what is a value experience for the self is found in relatedness to the other and is bound to have

"Culture and the Experience of Value," by Dorothy Lee. From A. H. Maslow, ed., *New Knowledge in Human Values* (New York: Harper & Row Publishers, Inc., 1959). Reprinted by permission of Harper & Row Publishers, Inc. The original, a slightly different version, was a paper delivered at the New Knowledge in Human Values Conference, Massachusetts Institute of Technology, Cambridge, Mass., October 4–5, 1957.

value for the related other also. Further, to experience value in the situation, the relation between self and other, self and surround, must be immediate. Labeling previous to experience, categorizing, analysis, assessment, calculation, measurement, evaluation, all erect barriers diminishing or even destroying true relatedness. This is to say that to provide a value experience, the relatedness must have the character of unconditional love.

What I refer to as *a* value is a part of the culture; and as cultures differ, so do values differ also, at least in specific form. Cultural values underlie individual choice and individual behavior; and they are known to us only through their manifestations, as expressed through the structure of the culture, the specific behavioral patterns, such as the seating arrangements, the ritual design, sometimes even the linguistic categories. Therefore, whether I am describing patterned behavior, or make mention of values specifically, I shall be referring to human values.

I

My thesis here is that cultures are structured in such a way as to maintain and enhance social value and, each in its own way, to furnish for the individual, situations rich in social value, and to develop in the individual sensitivity to value, and the capacity to experience value.

According to this thesis, the behavior patterns provided by the culture of a society furnish the form in which value will enter the experience of its members, and determine the degree and strength of this experience of value. The values of a culture are avenues through which relatedness is channeled. The avenues vary widely, but the variety is mainly one of form, depending on the individual style of each culture. In recent years, anthropologists, and particularly Clyde Kluckhohn, have pointed to the universality of certain basic human values. For example, Kluckhohn writes:

No society has ever approved of suffering as a good thing in itself. As a means to an end (purification or self-discipline), yes; as punishment—as a means to the ends of society, yes. But for itself—no. No culture fails to put a negative valuation upon killing, indiscriminate lying, and stealing within the in-group. There are important variations, to be sure, in the conception of the extent of the in-group and in the limits of toleration of lying and stealing under certain conditions. But the core notion of the desirable and nondesirable is constant across all cultures. Nor need we dispute the universality of the conception that rape or any achievement of sexuality by violent means is disapproved.

For Kluckhohn these values are universal because they "are founded, in part, upon the fundamental biological similarities of all human beings. They arise also out of the circumstance that human existence is invariably a social existence."

I agree with Kluckhohn up to a point. However, to my mind, the universality, or near universality, of these values also arises out of the fact that in these we find a cultural mediation of value itself. The values listed by Kluckhohn are a negative formulation of social value; implicit in them is the judgment that it is wrong to bring destruction, disruption, dissent, coercion, into the unit of relatedness. In these values, there is even a general agreement in form. I believe that also in the positive aspect, in the sense of multiplying value situations and infusing value into individual experience, cultures show similarity; but the forms vary so widely that the similarity is more difficult to recognize.

We have, for example, the Arapesh of New Guinea, who were visited by Margaret Mead in the thirties. The Arapesh terrain is mountainous, so rugged that there is almost no level land. The small garden plots might be separated from the hamlet by miles of difficult territory. The most economical way to cultivate them would have been to have one gardener working alone; yet up to six men would work on a small plot, often with their wives and children, traveling over forbidding territory from plot to distant plot, enjoying each other's society and the sharing of work. "The ideal distribution of food," writes Margaret Mead, "is for each person to eat food grown by another, eat game killed by another, eat pork from pigs that have been fed by people at . . . a distance." A man walked miles with his coconut saplings to plant them on the house sites of others, he gave his pigs to relatives in distant hamlets to feed and tend for him, he hunted only to give his kill away, since the lowest form of humanity was the man who ate his own kill, even one tiny bird. The system actually forbade a man to eat of his own kill; but it did not forbid him to give his pigs to his own wife to tend, or to plant all his trees by his own house. Taboo and preference, however, both went hand in hand toward creating a wide gap between ownership and possession: What a man possessed he did not own, what he owned he gave to another. This gap then provided continuing opportunities for experience in social value.

Thus it was ensured that, on the one hand, the Arapesh had little to eat, but also it meant that every mouthful that they consumed had been the medium of social participation, and contained social value.

Social value was channelled into experience through a variety of ways, regulations, attitudes, behavior patterns. Any surplus of food, for instance, however small, was always temporary as it was always the occasion for inviting others to a feast. The kinship system, again, was seen as something to be manipulated as a medium for discovering avenues of relatedness. And, quite often, the relationship with a given individual would be traced through a rambling route which brought in a large number of intermediate relatives.

Even incest regulations were phrased as having the function of enhancing relatedness. When Margaret Mead asked whether a man ever married his sister, she was met with incredulous amazement. Her informants inquired, in effect, "If we did so, where would we get brothers-in-law?" And, of course, to marry one's own sister instead of the sister of another man would deprive one of two sets of brothers-in-law, two wide-branching channels for relatedness and shared experience.

Participation in the experience of the other, actually in the self of the other, was facilitated again through the way in which relations between husband and wife, father and child were codified. A good husband was one who grew his wife, ideally from the time when she first came to his parents' home as a little girl. He grew his wife mainly by giving her food for which he was responsible—food which he had grown or killed himself; also, he helped her to grow unimpeded by his behavior, for example by refraining from intercourse until after she reached puberty. A good father grew his children in the same way. Together, throughout the period of pregnancy, husband and wife grew the child. Before and after the birth of the child, the food the father provided, what he did and what he refrained from doing, all went into growing the child. His time, his energy, his physical exertion, his good will and concern, his skill, his very self, became incorporated in his wife and children.

As Margaret Mead presents the Arapesh, social value so permeated their lives that it would have required deliberate effort to cut it out of experience. She describes how, even when a man was walking alone through the jungle, he was in a sense carrying his society with him, so that what he saw along the way was not a vine, a piece of wood, but rather a vine to be picked for Y's roof, a plank for R's house. And the walk he was taking most probably had reference to a social framework.

The Arapesh must have found great value through the structure of the situations in their culture, because these were maintained in the face of their serious interference with foodgetting. The Arapesh would have driven a welfare department or any efficiency expert completely mad. Their daily diet fell far below that needed for minimum subsistence by our dietary standard. Margaret Mead reports that they never ate their fill, that they always seemed hungry even during their feasts, which would have appeared pitifully meager yet these people persisted in arranging their working time uneconomically and in being prodigal with their presumably little energy. They managed in this way to include a maximum experience of social value in their lives.

In the culture of the Oglala Indians of this country, value was interpreted and infused into experience in an entirely different way, through an entirely different set of human values. Here relatedness was overtly recognized and sought as the ultimate value. It was indispensable for the growth and strengthening of a man to achieve relatedness with the manifestations of the Great Spirit—earth, plants, animals, stars, thunder, etc.—broadening in scope and intensifying through life. So the emphasis was on rigorous development of the self; but this was important only because a man was responsible for his social unit, or rather *as* his social unit, since he was an interpenetrating part of his camp circle, representing it in his person. Therefore, to enhance himself meant to enhance his unit.

Development of the individual in relatedness was initiated by the mother and eventually taken on by the growing boy. The mother initiated her unborn baby into relatedness with nature and continued to do so in various ways through his infancy. She took the very tiny baby out and merely pointed to natural manifestations, without labelling. Only after the baby experienced directly, only later, did she offer him concepts. She sang songs to him referring to the animals as his brothers, his cousins, his grandparents. Early in life he was also helped to develop sensitivity toward nature, so that he might be enabled to relate openly, without interference from what I think Dr. Suzuki called the *Ego*. Standing Bear writes: "Children were taught to sit still—and look when apparently there was nothing to see, and to listen intently when all seemingly was quiet" . . . and to "become conscious of life about us in its multitude of forms." Categorizing and logic are not absent from the culture but they come afterward. After the child has been initiated into acquaintance with nature, he is guided into using this as observed data on the basis of which he can draw conclusions. It is as if an individual is first encouraged to fall down and then helped to make a scientific study of gravitation. Logic did not mediate experience, but was bound up in experience. At the same time the growing individual was acquiring tremendous self-discipline, and training himself in hardihood, in skills, in endurance of incredible physical pain and danger. On the face of it, all this is self-centered; yet it was actually social because only through the strength and development of the individual could the social unit prosper, and only through personal enhancement could the individual be worthy of relationship with the multitude of manifestations of the Great Spirit.

On the surface, Arapesh and Oglala values were diametrically different. The Oglala valued what we call the manly, both in man and woman. The Arapesh valued that which Mead has called maternal. The Oglala foodgetting was impressively efficient; if they hunted in groups, it was for more effective results, not for the sake of being together. The Oglala individual often spent time alone; and he sought his religious experience ultimately in solitude, alone in the midst of the manifestations of the Great Spirit with whom he sought communion. Yet, in his person, he represented his camp circle; his prayer to Wakan Tanka, the Great Spirit, was: Help me that my people may live. And into the pipe he smoked to the Great Spirit at this time had been introduced with painstaking symbolism all the four groups of animals, the cardinal directions, the seasons, the times of day, the earth, the sky, the region below. At this time, while alone, with the pipe in his hand, the Oglala seeker represented the entire social unit, reaching out for communion with the entire universe.

II

In their different styles, the Arapesh and the Oglala cultures present relatedness as value. It is this which is ultimately at the base of individual choice, and it is participation in this which gives meaning to life. Now relatedness in this sense is possible only when the self is open to the other, to the surround; and cultures differ in the form in which they present the open self to the participant. In the Arapesh culture, I believe the open self is presupposed, and the emphasis is on furnishing, finding, creating a multiplicity of occasions for the exercise of the open self in transaction. The Oglala concentrate on enhancing the openness of the self, on the immediacy of apprehension; on broadening the field of transaction, on refining and intensifying the experience of the open self.

With the Wintu Indians, whose language I recorded, the open self is expressed in terms of interpenetration of the experience of self and other. For example, in a tale I recorded, a man, speaking of his sick son, added a suffix to the verb: *I am ill,* and now said, "I am ill my son": and later, "I am recovered my son." With the aid of this suffix, a chief haranguing his people about the coming of the Whites was quoted as saying: "You shall hunger your children, you shall hunger your horses." When this suffix occurred with a verb such as *I ate,* I found it easy to translate the phrase as "I fed my child." But here I was probably violating the meaning of the Wintu speaker. *I fed* presupposes a separate, bounded self acting upon another separate, bounded self; I did something, whether desired or not, *to* someone else. If there is consistency in the meaning of the suffix, I believe it must always be translated in such a way that it expresses some kind of immediate participation in the experience of the other; so that, I do not *feed my child,* but rather: "I eat in respect to my child," as: "I hunger in respect to my child," "I am ill in respect to my child." That is, I am open to the experience of my child. This is only one of the many cases where the linguistic forms as well as the cultural structure of the Wintu expresses their peculiar formulation of the openness of the self.

To say that the self is open is not to say that the self is fused with or submerged in the other. In all the cultures which I have studied, reference is made to a differentiated self. In the Wintu language for example, in addition to the personal pronouns, we have at least two suffixes whose function is to differentiate and emphasize the self; and, in the case which I cited above, the father who participated in the son's illness was named in distinction from the son. The Wintu did not use an *and* when they spoke of two or more individuals: In our terms, they would say not: John *and* Mary have arrived but: John Mary they have arrived. This may imply that the coming of John and the coming of Mary are not separate, to be joined by an *and;* yet John and Mary were clearly differentiated.

When I was in my teens, I was tortured by a question which I think would never have disturbed the Wintu or the Arapesh or the Oglala. If I dashed out to save a child from death or maiming at the risk of my own life, would I be doing it for *the child's* sake or for *my* sake? Would my act be altruistic or selfish? Upon which of these values would my chosen action be based? Would I be saving his life so that he could enjoy it, or only because I could not bear to live with myself if I did not try to save him? This question, of course, presupposed a conception of the self as closed, in limited, purposive interaction.

In a society where relatedness stems from the premise of the open self, such a question would be nonsense. In such societies, though the self and the other are differentiated, they are not mutually exclusive. The self contains some of the other, participates in the other, and is in part contained within the other. By this I do not mean what usually goes under the name of empathy. I mean rather that where such a concept of the self is operative, self-interest and other-interest are not clearly distinguished; so that what I do for my own good is necessarily also good for my unit, the surround, whether this is my family, my village, my tribe, my land, or even nature in general, the entire universe. So the Oglala Indian could concentrate his entire life on developing his self, through rigorous self-discipline and privation, through intense physical suffering, through the systematic sharpening of his senses and the refining of his sensitivity, thus making himself worthy of communion with nature, the manifestation of the Great Spirit, doing all this ultimately for the welfare of the camp circle. What he asked of Wakan Tanka, the Great Spirit, was: "Help me that my people may live," and, he could say at this time: "I am the people." Was this egoism or altruism?

I can say, "Help *me* that *my people* may live" only when the self is continuous with the other; and when this is so, whether I enhance myself, whether I expose myself to illness or pollution, whether I allow myself to deteriorate, in every case this is not a matter involving only myself, and it is not even a matter purely affecting others, but rather a situation shared by the other because I am to some extent the other.

A corollary to this view of the self is that, in respecting the other, the self is simultaneously respected. If the other is enjoyed in its totality, it means that the self must also be enjoyed. I cannot trust the other, value the other, unless I also love and value myself. In societies where the individual is ideally at one with, in harmony with, society, nature, the universe, we find that the self has tremendous value. So the Navaho, for example, valuing harmony and relatedness with the universe, believed that to assume the attitude of supplication or of gratitude toward the divine, was to devalue or humiliate the divine with whom he was to some degree identified. The Oglala man seeking power through communion with nature had (to quote from the autobiography of Standing Bear) "to prove to some bird or animal that he was a worthy friend. . . . The animal would thereafter observe and learn from the dreamer," and the dreamer also "should do likewise." The Oglala man who sought a vision was, in Standing Bear's words: "Humble without cringing, without loss of spirit. He always *faced* the Powers in prayer; he never grovelled on the earth, but with face lifted to the sky he spoke straight to his Mystery."

III

Not all cultures afford a multiplicity of value situations; and not all encourage immediacy of relationship between self and other. If systems of value are specific cultural mediations of value itself, then I think they can be assessed and judged according to their effectiveness in making value available for human experience. To use Dr. Hartman's term, according to the degree in which they fulfill their concept. For instance, I believe that totalitarianism, wherever it is found, is a misrepresentation and a wrong mediation of social value. In totalitarianism, the self is neither differentiated nor valued; and, when this is so there can be no true transaction in relatedness; that which is afforded as an experience in social value is a travesty.

I spoke earlier of the Oglala individual who enhanced his own self because in so doing he enhanced his group. However, one of the ways in which he did this was through going on the warpath against the Utes and others, stealing horses, scalping, killing. Hardihood was a value, self-discipline as a duty to the tribe was a value; and going on the warpath was the ultimate exercise of valor, hardihood, self-discipline. Yet the ideal of the Oglala was eventual relatedness to all, harmony with all the manifestations of the Great Spirit and, therefore, harmony with all men. So the warrior was actually going against the ultimate value of the society in satisfying the specific more superficial formulation.

There are also societies having cultural systems in which we find a conception of the self as completely bounded, and where the values strengthen the barriers which separate the self from the surround. In such societies, only mediated experience is encouraged, valued, and recognized as valid; and the other is not experienced as *this,* that is, in immediate relatedness, but is apprehended only cognitively in analysis. According to *my* view of value, a society having such values makes it difficult or impossible for the individual to experience value. What I judge to be a good system of values enables the individual to fill his life with value situations, and to be open to the experience of value. It enables him to value himself as well as the other, to develop himself while developing the other and to relate himself in a transaction which enhances the value of both self and other.

AUTONOMOUS MOTIVATION

I have called this chapter "Autonomous Motivation" only because I could find no other term which would communicate what I want to say before I develop it at length. I hope to show that where there is full engagement of the individual in his life, he is invited to act rather than motivated to act. I shall speak of a view of motivation which is gaining ground in recent years. In my own case, it was arrived at through work with non-Western cultures and it is original only insofar as the journey I made, from departure to arrival, was my own.

In writing this chapter I encountered great difficulty because all the words at hand, and all the concepts they represented, were relevant to a view of motivation which I have found inadequate to cover all the data encountered. In describing cultural situations which have forced me to reconsider my old view, I have had to use negatives when I was referring to something whose very peculiarity was affirmation. I have had to go against my long training in restrained and measured scholarly prose. The words I sometimes chose are deplorable because what they refer to—the uninhibited, the impulsive—is itself unacceptable. But, in fact, there were far too few such words available to me. So I have had to describe that which is without limit in terms which imply limit.

At first I saw such situations only in the non-Western cultures I was studying, perhaps because the entire structure of those

"Autonomous Motivation," by Dorothy Lee. From *Journal of Humanistic Psychology*, Fall 1961, pp. 12–22. Reprinted by permission.

societies was based on a non-Western assumption of "motivation." I have later come to see that this was true also of the people around me in my own society; I saw that the official view of motivation—which I had accepted—and the conception of the self which this presupposed had blurred my vision, so that I did not see what was there.

When I first started studying anthropology, I had accepted the notion that man behaved in response to basic needs. Man's activities were presented to me as economic or, at any rate, as leading to the satisfaction of needs. When they were religious, even religion was presented to me as a means to an end—usually to an economic end—with pre-imagined, hoped-for results, furnishing the activity literally with an end, a finish. With the years, the social sciences have provided me with a variety of theories of motivation. Man was motivated to satisfy basic needs, or to reduce tension, or to respond to an externally applied stimulus: or he was propelled by some inner drive.

To my mind, all these theories differed only in specifics. Essentially they all viewed man as inert, driven, or prodded, or otherwise dependent on a furnished motivating power. But what I found when I read about "primitive cultures" contradicted all this. The behavior I saw was often non-utilitarian or even anti-utilitarian; it was often deliberately wasteful of materials and energy and consciously inefficient—to use a term which has relevance only within my own framework of concepts. For such and similar behavior, the social scientist provided me with motivation, such as prestige, for instance. But, by this time, I was wary of Western explanations. It seemed to me that the Western social scientist actually described how *he* felt, how *he* behaved—with *his* Western need for sensible moderation, for weighing the consequences of his actions, for rigid, limiting logic and admiration for restraint and reasonableness. He said to himself, "If I were a Kwakiutl or a Trobriander, why would I be doing this?" But the fact is that he was not a Kwakiutl. In fact, I am not even sure that he told me how he as a person felt in this situation and what propelled him to action. I rather think he told me how he ought to feel, in accordance with the theories he held.

At any rate, the data from other societies questioned all this. For instance, I started with the view that man acted to satisfy basic needs and when he could not be expected to act directly so as to satisfy these needs, then he had to be stimulated in some other way. Reward had to be dangled before him, a stimulus had to prod him, or later a drive had to push him; or the discomfort of tension moved him to act to achieve a resolution or reduction of the tension. Yet there were the Eskimo, who ate when they were hungry and fully satisfied their hunger—acting, I imagine, according to the traditional theory of motivation—but then kept on eating unreasonably for many hours while the food lasted. Why? Conversely, there were the hungry Arapesh, who instead of being properly motivated to work so as to satisfy their hunger, instead of spending time and energy in producing more food so that they would not be continually hungry, wasted the larger part of their time and effort in a variety of undertakings which resulted merely in a virtuosity of non-utilitarian social intercourse.

In fact, in a variety of ways, I saw people of other cultures going to absurd lengths of effort, to extremes of behavior completely inexplicable when set within a "reasonable" framework of views about human behavior. I found people like the Kwakiutl, who worked outrageously, with vigor and involvement, beyond any crying need to satisfy hunger; people who collected stupendous amounts of oil only to burn it in a gigantic public conflagration, in a fantastic game of trying to unseat their visitors who had come purposely to engage in this sport. I read Malinowski's account of the Trobrianders who undertook laborious and fearful expeditions involving the careful working out of a variety of magical performances and the observation of greatly depriving taboos. These expeditions meant cutting down large trees with stone implements and taking them to the shore without vehicles and without roads, necessitated building sea-going canoes, the collecting of provisions, and striking out into witch-infested waters. They were time-consuming, effort-demanding; and brought in no food, no clothing, or shelter—nothing but some "ornaments" which did not even adorn. In fact, most of them could not or would not be worn; and probably would not be possessed for more than a year. I could not see these people propelled by any of the basic needs. And what drives could be strong enough to push the Kwakiutl and the Trobrianders into such extremes of exertion? What stimulus could be massive enough to result in this response?

Such questions forced me to discard all theories of motivation with which I was acquainted and to see what I could find for myself. The needs, drives, and tensions which I had been offered as sources of behavior in our culture were too bound by the limits of our own reasoning to account for the exorbitant behaviors that I found in other cultures. In fact, the whole list of needs and drives was to my mind irrelevant when I tried to see it in connection with these behaviors. Hunger does motivate, but meagerly, within limits;

its satiation forms a rigid ceiling. Hunger goads me as I goad a reluctant animal which responds up to a point, compelled into moving a required amount. But what explains the running, the skipping, the bounding? Why does my goat leap over the highest "obstacles" in the path instead of taking the easy effortless way around them as I do?—obviously these obstacles invite rather than obstruct. Why does the Eskimo, after he satisfies hunger, eat food which he has risked his life to get—without thought of tomorrow's hunger? Why did the Trobrianders grow, with such unreasonable exertion, twice as many yams as they needed, doing a great amount of hard work which did not go into increasing or bettering or ensuring the yield—"unnecessary" work; and then have magic made so that these yams should rot undisturbed and uneaten in the yamhouse?

Once I decided that I needed a fresh theory, I saw that people in all the societies which I studied exerted themselves—often to unimaginable lengths—but their efforts might or might not result in food or shelter or prestige. It seemed as if the exertion itself, expanded within a meaningful situation, was sufficient in itself.

When I looked around me in this country, I did not see such absurdity of exertion at first glance. I saw people preferring to ride rather than walk, to push a button rather than light a stove, to turn on an automatic washing machine rather than scrub clothes. I saw people responding to the stimulus of profit, working harder and longer for more pay. Yet I also saw these same people working even harder, beyond profit and beyond pay. I saw women inventing new stitches to make their knitting more engrossing and demanding of more alertness; and I saw them devising more intricate and laborious cooking to do on their push-button stoves.

All around me I saw people who work to earn money to buy themselves the opportunity to exert themselves for no profit, beyond any imaginable limit; unreasonable, without calculating risk or effort or profit, in danger to limb and life itself; attempting to climb inaccessible cliffs and peaks, skiing, shooting rapids, swimming beyond the limits of safety. Occasionally they did this in public—perhaps seeking prestige—but much more often they did it in obscurity.

I saw all this most clearly in connection with our own educational process. This was when my son, a high school freshman, took up tennis. He had been a text book paradigm of the theory of motivation which I had held. According to his teachers and the school authorities, he was a model student, fulfilling all require-ments and meeting all obligations. He carried out all his assignments competently, completing them acceptably on time. In every school situation, he moved until he bumped his head against the ceiling of his goal: the reasonable expectations of his teachers and the established requirements for an *A*. His mind was flabby; he was bored and listless. He did not want to get up in the morning because there was nothing to get up for.

Then he discovered tennis. This had an inviting horizon—a horizon which could never stop him because it retreated as he moved. No contrived incentive had to be furnished, no fixed grade insured a reasonable effort, no defined achievement put an end to his effort. Tennis invited him to unlimited exertion. Now on Sundays he got up at daybreak so as to have a long time at the tennis courts without a break for meals, dressed unbecomingly in sweat clothes against the cold drizzle of late winter. Paying no heed to discomfort or the passage of time, he played far into exhaustion.

What motivated him? He was certainly not motivated by the need to succeed competitively. I watched him in a junior championship. He was apathetic and sluggish, engaged only to a minimum; his opponent did not offer him strong competition. It was a poor game and he did not enjoy it. He was not glad or proud of his "success." Conversely, whenever he could, he chose for himself partners who were bound to defeat him. He chose them because they gave him a good game. What was he seeking? What he was seeking was an opponent—and I use this term in its literal sense of someone who is opposite—who would draw from him the full exercise of all that was in him; one who would evoke him, not push or compel him, to an answering response of exertion beyond known limits. The partners he liked usually defeated him. Yet he chose them because they invited him to actualize all his capacities —his coordination, his split-second judgment, his footwork, his skill, his imagination, his planning—all of these focused upon the one instant of hitting the tennis ball. He sought for a partner one who would engage his whole being to full commitment.

You will say that this is because he liked sports and not books, but I believe this is not so. He went to his school with a passion for mathematics. He was filled with an urgent inquiry into logic and values and metaphysics; he wanted to know how we know what we know, and what is man. But the school could not recognize urgency, and felt responsible to protect him against the enormity of his own appetite for knowledge and exploration. Besides, they had on hand a system of organized, externally applied motivations for the students, since the filling of school assignments could not be left to the compelling force of basic needs. So they stopped his immoderate appetite by feeding him what was moderate and good for him, what was appropriate for a boy of his age. For his clamorous inquiry they substituted their concept of what an educated man should know; or the so-called need for achievement, which could be satisfied when one's limited goal had been achieved. If his urgency had been recognized and encouraged, instead of being firmly fenced in—if the view of motivation as depending on needs and drives and external stimuli had not been substituted for the striving of the human spirit, I believe he would have been truly as alive in school as he was on the tennis court. Actually, he himself was aware of the constricting effect of set goals and chose to go to a college without grades, where his inquiry is gushing freely and tennis has taken second place.

Eventually, I came to form another view of man's behavior. I saw man as moving rather than motivated, as thrusting forward, striving, aspiring. As I said above, others also have come to this view of man. The biologist, Edmund Sinnott, means something of this sort when he speaks of the "inner urgencies that guide behavior," and when he says of man, "there comes bubbling up in him a 'host of desires' . . . his cravings for beauty, his moral aspirations, his love of his fellows." Another biologist, Ludwig von Bertalanffy, speaks of this when he says, "the organism should not be considered as a responding machine but rather as primary activity . . . primary behavior is continuous . . ." Gordon Allport refers to this as "propriate striving," which could distinguish itself from other forms of motivation in that, however beset by conflict, it makes for "unification of personality." Abraham Maslow speaks of the value of being fully human, and of the urge of the self to flex its muscles, so to speak; and he, as well as Kurt Goldstein, speaks of man as striving toward self-actualization.

What struck me about what I call striving, or thrust, was that the behavior in which it eventuated was prodigal, exuberant, unpredictable in its reach. I now saw man as spontaneously eager to exert himself to the utmost of his capacities in his striving to be fully human. And immediately I was appalled at the niggardliness of my terms, and of the concepts which they named. The "utmost" I just used merely pushes the limit out a little further; the fullest is still limited by what it fills. I can fill my cup to its utmost limit, but that is only to the known lip. If I speak of brimming over, of excess or exorbitance, all my terms refer to concepts which take account of measure and limit. Yet I have to use these terms, though they are in contradiction to what I say. In fact, I believe that lack of limit—infinitude—is a necessary dimension of this propriate striving, thus differentiating it absolutely from motivation whose quality is finitude and limit. Thus, the thrust can be so exuberant as to bring down the criticism of the observer who will speak of improvidence, or the inability to resist one's impulses; or, as a participant, will worry at the childishness of people who cannot be taught rationing, or cannot realize the necessity for forced marches.

The exuberance of which I speak is most obvious in situations where we ourselves would have been moved to calculation and measure. Among people who are constantly on the brink of starvation, for instance, hospitality may be exercised to the point of what we could call madness. Consider, for instance, Thesiger's accounts of the Arabs of the Empty Quarter whom he visited some ten years ago. There is his description of the occasion when he and his five companions met an encampment of Bedu in this most desolate of deserts. These people had no tent, no blankets, no headdresses, no shirts, nothing but their ragged loincloths to spread over themselves in the freezing weather of the desert night. They had no food except the milk of their camels and this they pressed on their sudden uninvited guests, brooking no refusal; yet they had had nothing to eat or drink for a day, and would have nothing for another twenty-four hours. This is excessive giving, beyond the limits of common sense or rationality.

For that matter, their entire way of living was beyond the bounds of reasonable common sense. Thesiger reports that at this time the oil fields were in need of workers, who would be paid large sums for doing nothing except sit in the shade and guard a dump. Yet these Bedu resisted all invitation—I will not say temptation; it would have tempted *me* in their place, but it obviously was no temptation to them—to this easy way of earning a living. They lived in appalling discomfort. They went hungry, cold, exhausted from hard travelling by day and from unrefreshing nights disturbed by the need to move about to get some warmth. They were in constant danger of death from starvation, from thirst, from camel-raiders.

Thesiger speaks of hiring a pack camel whose owner was ready to walk across the desert with him. This man had worn out the soles of his feet on the journey he had just completed, and was prepared to walk on raw flesh on the harsh floor of the desert. This is absurd, particularly since he could have earned money easily working in a garden in a village.

These people chose to live in this way; and no Western explanation can encompass the effulgence which gave rise to and supported this choice.

In one form or other, I find this exuberant exertion in most of the cultures I know. There are differences, however. Each culture contains its own definition of what it is to be fully human, has its own areas where man is invited to limitless exertion, and furnishes its own peculiar situations which call forth man's exertion. To be fully human means to be completely organically continuous with one's social unit—as among the Nyakyusa of Tanganyika, where the people exert themselves in learning and performing meticulously the minutely detailed and intricate practices which, for instance, will make a woman at one with the lineage of her husband, or a newly conceived embryo continuous with the body of his father. If, to be a man fully meant to be a gardener—as it did among the Trobrianders whom Malinowski visited—then a man went to all sorts of (to us) unnecessary and inexplicable lengths in performing his gardening.

If, as I believe to be the case in our own culture at present, there is no official recognition of exuberance, then the human spirit burgeons beyond the official stricture. At present, for instance, we do not give sanction to effulgence, to gushing behavior without calculation of measure or risk—to excess. Officially, we ask for the calculable, the graspable. We aspire to a set ceiling. (See, for instance, David Riesman's *The Found Generation*.) Full humanness for us means no spilling over, no bursting through the bounds of measure and prediction. Yet—unofficially—outside the recognized structure of our culture the human spirit even in our present-day society does thrust beyond the limits set by the measure, and spills over into activities of absurd exertion and commitment such as the ones I mentioned above.

Another characteristic of thrust which I found was that it could not come forth in isolation; it existed in an open system of transaction. In every culture I studied, I found that if man was not "motivated"; that is, if he was not prodded into moving, he had to be invited to thrust forward. Cultural systems, affording man his place in the universal whole, furnished a variety of situations (to use a phrase which I shall have to contradict later) for calling forth man's exertion. I shall speak here of only one such system which I find in a variety of forms among the Indians and the Eskimo of this continent.

I believe that generally, among these people, man was viewed as a collaborator with the rest of nature, or the universe, in building the world of experience. I have found this to be so, at any rate, among those cultures which have been studied intensively enough to uncover man's view of his place in the universe. For instance, such a view seems to be underlying the verbal structure of the Navaho language. Here we have verbal forms which indicate that rollingness, or flyingness through the air, pre-exist as potential, or a design, in certain objects. A man does not *cause* a ball to roll; he releases its predisposition to roll, or actualizes the potential to roll, or puts the rollingness into operation. (I am profoundly aware of the inadequacy of all these phrases I have used just now; there are no such concepts in American culture, and all the words that this culture provides me with are inadequate and, in fact, *wrong* when I use them to present what I am trying to present.) Such a picture of man in the universe is clearly presented in the language of the Wintu Indians of California. Here the primary verbal stem refers to a world, a universe, that neither exists nor does not exist. We might say that it refers to the nature of things, a nature which is not realized because the things themselves do not exist; the situations have not come to be and may never come to be. Only at the instant when man experiences these do they come into existence—into history. The experiential or existential stem of the verb is derivative from this other stem. When man speaks with the aid of this stem, he asserts existence through his own experience of it. And it is only through his doing—through his decisive act or his act of will—that the world to which the primary stem refers can have concrete existence. This dialogue between the idea of the universe or the potential of the universe, and man's experience, runs through the entire verbal system, and perhaps through the entire linguistic structure.

With the Hopi Indians, we find it systematically expressed in their "Hopi Way." Here there was a pre-established universal order, a design; but it needed man's cooperation to become actualized. The course of the sun was set between winter solstice and summer solstice; but the sun could not move between these two solstices unless man cooperated. The land could not thaw to allow for planting, unless man translated the design into actuality.

Man's part in all this was to work—both in a technical sense and also in a religious sense through his ceremonials. Through ceremonials the sun was enabled to move from stage to stage, the corn was enabled to grow along its given cycle of growth. When he cleared the fields, when he dug and planted and weeded, when he sang to the growing corn to make it happy, and when he worked his corn ceremonial, man was cooperating with the corn to enable it to follow its course. To do this a Hopi needed to put himself through a long—in fact, an endless—educational process. He had to train his body, he had to learn to endure pain and cold and hunger and thirst. He had to learn technical processes to get detailed knowledge about the corn and its ways; and also he had to grow himself into a person who could carry out the necessary ceremonials. For instance, he had to learn to empty his mind from all dissonance and anxiety, from all evil thoughts. He had to discipline himself strongly, so that he could eventually concentrate on thinking good and peaceful thoughts only. Some men went further than others along this Hopi way. After the training of childhood, which *did* include punishment, all went eventually along this way without external coercion, in answer to the invitation to bring the design into human history.

This kind of picture of man's share in the universe emerged for the Eskimo, also, in a recent study by Paul Riesman. These people show a gusto for life—that is, their own way of life—which is difficult for us to comprehend. In fact, Western society was concerned to the point of making an effort to "ease the lot" of the Eskimo, thereby probably destroying the meaning of life for them. And it was easy to see them as people in need of help. Here were people for whom sudden disaster was commonplace, an everyday matter of living; people for whom pending starvation was a reality to be encountered at any time, people who froze to death, murdered, or were murdered with apparently slight provocation, were mauled to death by polar bears, fell into crevasses and were killed, overturned in their kayaks and were drowned. Their lives were so full of such hardships that it is incredible that anyone could have endured them, let alone chosen to endure them.

And yet these people have repeatedly been reported as being sorry for the White man because he had to live a different kind of life. In fact, some forty years ago, when one of them visited New York and came back to report on its large population, he was thought to be lying because his hearers could not believe that such a large number of people would choose to live this way when they could have lived in an Eskimo way.

This zest for (Eskimo) life, this readiness to endure hardship and encounter mortal danger, is called forth apparently through the part which a person finds for himself in the universal scheme. The Eskimo is a collaborator with the rest of the universe in creating the Eskimo world of existence.

For the Eskimo the universe is thought, but man only has the capacity to think. Yet man cannot think unless thought enters him, and thought cannot exist unless man thinks it. If I say, then, that thought exists outside man, every one of the words I use is wrong because I use them in the context of my culture where man is complete in himself, the universe is complete in itself, and thought either exists or does not exist. For the Eskimo, thought outside man does not have existence, it hovers on the brink of existence; in fact it is not thought, it does not exist, it is not outside, since the universe itself contains man and man is not man completely without the so-called outside.

Now this incompletion except in mutual collaboration—this interdependence for very existence—furnishes the equivalent of what we call motivation. Man is constantly invited to make actual both the existence of the world and his own existence. At the moment when he thinks, at the moment when he gives existence to the potential thought which is outside him (thought which is potential only insofar as man is ready and striving to give it actuality); at this moment man and the universe come into existence. Thought has now become a "think," to use Paul Riesman's term.

All events come into being in this way through man's collaboration; they have existed as thoughts outside man until man has brought them into history. And if man is to create a strong full situation, he has to do this with full humanity; he has to meet the universe with all his being strained to its utmost limits or, I should say, beyond any pre-conceivable limit. Now this in our own culture would be seen as motivation; here it is human striving in response to evocation which takes the form of a call to create one's world in collaboration. This is what is behind his urge to learn without end, to discipline himself, and to endure without limit.

And, in fact, to live his life in the Arctic, an Eskimo had to have a high development of skills, of perceptiveness and sensitivity of alertness. For instance, a man travelling through a dense snow storm had to know where, within the vast expanse, to dig his heel to uncover the two-inch track of the sled which went by before the storm. What multitude and variety of perceptions, what wealth of detailed knowledge, went into this one discovery, I cannot imagine; and the ethnographers themselves could not find out. A man had to grow in self-discipline until he could remain motionless at a seal hole for three or four days at a time, "feet planted together, head down, bottom high, forced by the seal's acute hearing to maintain absolute silence," and to do this while fully and passionately engaged, gazing with intensity, alert to the tiniest movement. He had to be ready and able to build an igloo in a blinding and smothering blizzard, imperturbable in the face of what was catastrophic to his White companion, without disorganizing haste, gently prodding the ground with his harpoon to find the proper snow, carefully cutting blocks with precision and speed, trimming lightly and accurately; and then, while his White companion huddled in the igloo in fear and misery, he had to be able to go out again into the blizzard, as a matter of course, to dig up the snow-buried dogs and feed them.

All this was an aspect of collaboration in building the world; it was all part of being Eskimo. When they lived a non-Eskimo life of ease, de Poncins describes the people as apathetic. He speaks about them at the trading post, where "they had warmth, they had biscuits, they had tea . . . They are dull, sullen, miserable . . . But open wide the door, fling them into the blizzard and they come to. Now they are Inuk, men pre-eminently."

I have not been indulging in an exercise in cultural relativity here. Though this view of man is so foreign to our own official culture that our language itself cannot be used to express it; actually, this view of man as invited to collaboration has been gaining ground for many years. When Dewey spoke of the transaction between buyer and seller, he was describing something like the Eskimo world. Buyer and seller are not buyer and seller, except insofar as they create each other in the process of transaction. I am not a buyer unless you are willing to sell to me. Conversely, you can become a seller only insofar as I am ready to buy.

There is a further dimension to this however. This is something which my son pointed out to me when I told him how I had described his tennis playing in the first part of this paper. He pointed out that he did not "play a game of tennis" against a competitor. There was no game to play. The two partners collaborated to create the game. The effort beyond calculable limit, the training in skills, the development of imagination, the boundless exertion, all these grew naturally out of the striving to help create a good game. And the choice of a strong competitor grew also out of this. If success came, it was welcome but it was secondary. To be motivated by the need for success in choosing a partner would have been to make the creation of the game itself incidental only.

The game of tennis is one of many situations in our culture which are so structured as to evoke the putting forth of effort, energy, exertion through an invitation to collaborate. Most of these situations, however, are outside the official framework of our society. For many years now, for instance, our artists, our musicians, our writers have been proceeding on this basis. As Koestler puts it, "The artist's aim is to turn his audience into accomplices." And, speaking of the author, Virginia Woolf says to her reader, "Be his fellow worker and accomplice."

I have directed my attention to motivation here largely because of the increasing concern in the schools with "under-achievement" and with "under-development of the capacity to learn." I have attempted to say in this chapter that the theory of motivation which we have applied generally in the schools does motivate, but only up to a limit. If the full capacity of the individual is to be tapped and encouraged toward development, we have to have a new view to operate on a new basis.

The basis which I have been describing in this paper, the strong invitation to the individual to collaborate in creating his situation—in this case his educational situation—has been progressively eliminated from the schools in this century.

We have seen competition only as competitive success, as leading to harmful comparative evaluation of the human being; and much of it was exactly this and was rightly expelled from the school situation. We saw achievement only as a pawn in the winning of conditional love, or as a bid for approval. As such it was undesirable and harmful, and was eliminated; at any rate, at the policy-making level. We failed to see achievement as the end product of spontaneously entered exertion and discipline as the enjoyed performance of carefully learned skills. And we failed to see the necessity for a competitor as collaborator in creating the situations which would call forth this unmeasured exertion, this chosen self-discipline and learning; and, in fact, there were no situations to create, as they were furnished ready-made.

In the beginning I said that I was not speaking of autonomous motivation. I have tried to show that I speak of striving and thrust instead, and that an individual, if he is to strive with all his capacity, is not completely autonomous; he needs to see himself as collaborating.

AUTONOMY AND COMMUNITY

In this chapter, I shall be using the terms of my title, familiar terms, to refer to something unfamiliar, something that I have to explain and whose presence I have to demonstrate; something seldom recognized and not readily found in our society. I shall be speaking of autonomy, which, far from rooting itself in rebellion and independence from community, depends for its very existence upon community and the individual's sense of community. And when I use the term *autonomy*, community will always be present by implication, in transaction with the autonomous individual, always only one end of a transaction, incomplete in itself, and incomprehensible by itself.

It is very difficult to write about this, because I am immediately faced by the situation around me. Surely, we must learn to question the authority of community before we can achieve individuality? The autonomous individuals in my acquaintance are people who rebelled against their families, or their schools; who decided for themselves against the plans and advice of others. They have tried to, perhaps even managed to, wash out of themselves even the sense of community, freeing themselves of its hampering tug. They are independent people.

And in our society, autonomy does seem to be the same as independence, independence from community. But this is true of a society which at the very beginning conceives of community and

"Autonomy and Community," by Dorothy Lee. From *Humanitis,* I, no. 2, 1965, 147–59. Reprinted by permission.

individual autonomy as separate units, at best delineating separate and meticulously non-interfering orbits for them. Under such circumstances, when there is infringement, there is trouble; the individual is violated, encroached upon. In his turn the individual may work havoc upon the community into whose orbit he trespasses. When the principle of non-interference is respected, the situation may range from armed hostility, the strategy of the cold war, to what we have called permissiveness, which at its purest is non-involvement.

The rebels I have known have turned against one or the other of these situations—against the first because it continually smothered and enslaved them; against the second, with more difficulty, because it was a negative, it was an absence, because it failed them. And in both kinds of cases, to my mind, these people could rebel at all, could set out on a search for autonomy, only because somewhere in their lives they discovered true community; only when they discovered a friend, a teacher, a counselor, a priest, a wife who recognized their dignity, who valued and trusted them.

I shall not defend my position here. I would spend myself in windy exposition, or lose myself in a bog of polemics. Instead, I shall present a society where autonomy and community flourish strongly and indubitably, and where each presupposes the presence of the other for its very definition. I am tempted to let the presentation speak for itself, but I know I shall not leave it alone. Is it that I do not trust my readers to hear for themselves? I think so. I come to this material from long experience of dealing with the material of cultures other than my own. So I will be pointing out as well as presenting, and perhaps even giving my own interpretation of the phenomena. I hope my comments will be clearly comments, allowing the reader to see the unaffected situation.

For my presentation I shall draw on autobiographic accounts of people who were born some hundred years ago. They are Dakota Indians, who speak of a way of life which was destroyed, to a large extent, under the impact of White conquest and occupation. If I mention mostly men and boys, it is because only men of this period left us their autobiographies.

What do I mean by autonomy? If I am talking about my own society I usually describe autonomy in negative terms, in terms of non-interference by the community, in terms of allowing the individual to have experience which has not first been filtered for him, ideas and conclusions which have not been prefabricated, values which are not gauged by the expectations of others. In my own talk, I find myself using such words as inviolate, or unadulterated; all negative. If I have achieved all this with my children or my students, all I have achieved is a no-wrong, a nothingness. I have not set up obstacles, I have not prevented them from being autonomous; does this therefore mean that now they can, or will want to, proceed autonomously? What I have done is to reach bedrock, clean of all the garbage; a starting point. But unless I redefine, unless I radically change my notion of autonomy, I am not now, at bedrock, on common ground with the Dakota; there is a deep split between us. To reach their bedrock, I have to leap over a bottomless split. Because the notion in my society is that now, free of all interference, autonomy will flourish; it is a capacity of the individual. All it needs to come to actuality, is to be left alone.

What I mean to affirm about autonomy will emerge from my presentation. At this point, I shall give only a sketchy definition. By autonomy I mean minimally the personal quality whereby an individual can and will choose his own course of action, and chooses to experience rather than allowing experience to happen to him. Such an individual sees with his own eyes, what is there; not what he has been led to expect to be there. He recognizes his own feelings and deals with experience in terms of these, taking them into account. My definition then includes authenticity, and more than that. It includes an act of involvement at every step in existence. For me, seeing "this" in its purity, as it reveals itself—not lazily, with dormant senses, what I know must be there—; such seeing, is more than authentic seeing. It is effortful, dynamic, imbued with the energy of urgency. If English has a word which conveys this thrust of involvement, which requires unmeasured and uncalculated, in fact absurd exertion, I do not know it. Yet I have to refer to this thrust, because for me this, the tremendous step of overcoming the lurking resistance to becoming engaged in piercing experience, this also is a necessary dimension of autonomy. Without it, I can see no autonomous behavior or experience. Autonomy then would be just a waiting quality; not an act, not a choosing to act.

To act autonomously is not easy. It requires a break in the quiescence. It cries for my effort, my attention, the concentration of me, my self. It is not a giving-in to an idle whim, or to any whim. As the term implies, the self (autos) is in charge, is regulating (nomy); but here I must understand this without the isolating split between subject and object, controlling and controlled.

Until recently, I thought of autonomy as a capacity, born in every individual. When I saw around me the prevalence of inauthentic experience and even the preference for the inauthentic, I felt that this was so because within the cultural framework of these people, there was a systematic ignoring of the capacity for autonomy, until by later childhood the individual had lost the capacity. I was sure that babies came into the world with the urge to exert their own selves. I saw them seeking to exercise their muscles without limit; sucking with all their strength, expressing limitless outrage with all the force of kicking legs, plunging arms, straining muscles, while roaring with all the capacity of lungs and vocal chords. I saw them pursuing their curiosity with all their senses, enduring discomfort, exerting. At no point were they "sparing" themselves. Then one day I found them insisting on being driven to school, on being told the answers, on being furnished with passive entertainment. I saw them lazily doing what was expected of them by teachers or peers, or at most succumbing to whim; not choosing. It was obvious to me that their culture had done this to them, had deprived them of their autonomy and destroyed the very capacity for autonomy.

Now I have decided that this was a wrong conclusion, based on a false premise. I realized that the infants that delighted me with their strong autonomy were the loved infants, evoked by cherishing community, responding to mothers and others who cared. Now I saw the other infants also, the unloved infants, the ones whose tentative acts of emergence met with no response; the infants that René Spitz writes about, the ones in foundling homes throughout the world. These do not roar and kick with outrage; in fact, I doubt that they feel outrage. They whimper instead of roaring; they make vague lazy movements instead of kicking lustily. Their behavior is automatic, not autonomous. These are infants without community, and with no capacity for autonomy. There is no interference to stop its emergence; there is almost no one around to interfere.

I came to the conclusion that autonomy existed only as design in the newborn individual; perhaps a right, to be recognized by community, a readiness to be afforded an opportunity. But not a capacity. The potency which will transform the pending into a capacity has to come in transaction with the enabling community. And community itself has to be felt; there has to be a sense of community.

And so I come to the bedrock of the Dakota, to a situation where I have to mention community and autonomy in the same breath. For these unimaginably autonomous, self-dependent, strong individuals, community was an ever-present reality. Even at the time when a man, alone on a hill-top, sought for days to establish his own relationship with his God, to earn the relationship autonomously, even then, community was a part of him, he was serving his people. Conversely, as Standing Bear puts it, "In serving my tribe, I was serving myself. If I failed in duty, I simply failed to meet a test of manhood. . . ." The community, on its part, took everything that I have been struggling to express and explain for granted, not to be talked about or defended; self-evident. Of course an infant had dignity and worth, to be recognized and valued; therefore, naturally, he had the right to autonomy. The right to and readiness for autonomy were as unquestioned as his right to his mother's milk or his readiness to suck. In such a situation, there was no strategy of non-interference, either to protect the individual, or to protect the well-intentioned community from its own urge to violate. In such a situation, the sentence I have just written is nonsense.

In fact, much in the life of these people bewildered and confounded me, until I gave up my original definition of autonomy. I admired the way they brought up their children to be completely autonomous. For instance, a mother would take out her baby and point birds or bushes or rocks to him, focus this attention, but not name them. This was fine; I liked it. This was unfiltered experience. Later, when the baby was beginning to talk, the mother gave these things names. "Whenever I heard the song of a bird, she would tell me what bird it came from," writes Eastman. Good. But the mother does not stop here; she goes on: "He says he has just found something good to eat." Or: "He is singing for his little wife." Isn't she putting her ideas into the baby's head? Isn't she interfering with autonomous experience? Then, the boys and mature men, whose autonomy leaves me agape, are expected to obey and do obey; boys perform terrific self-initiated feats, fired by the desire to please their fathers (but should they not try to please themselves, instead?).

Parents offer unsolicited advice, information, directions, and their sons take no offense. Instead of letting their children discover the path of self-discipline through trial and error, floundering along, adults set tasks for them. Men and women perform little pampering services for their sons who are perfectly capable of doing them themselves. Yet I see that autonomy remains undimmed. This I particularly resent as I remember with regret all the tender services that I prevented myself from performing for my own children, for the sake of fostering their autonomy.

How can I do justice to Dakota autonomy in my words? It was such an integral part of the human being that it has survived the disaster of conquest, the breakdown of the culture, the consequent despair and demoralization. Rosalie Tax, working with Dakota and other Indians who were attending college, that is, who had attended

White man's schools and lived in the ways of the Whites, found that among these, some hundred years after the birth of Standing Bear, one man would not address another whose back was turned; because, how can he know that the man is ready and willing to be addressed unless he can look at him, and observe the expression of his face?, unless he senses consent? As the speaker has the right to choose to speak, so does the hearer have the right to choose to hear.

In the days which Standing Bear speaks of, decisions of the council were announced to the band, but no orders were given, and no one would conceive of enforcing a decision upon another, except in the case of the communal hunt when, to go hunting individually would mean to frighten the herd away and bring disaster to the entire community. In these days, when the decision was made to move camp, with hundreds of people involved, women, children, the old, the crippled, dogs, horses, possessions, no one told anyone what to do. "Each did his own duty without orders." (Apparently, each knew his duty clearly and wanted to carry it out.) If a family did not want to move, it did not join the rest; the decision was respected. These people looked appalled upon the Whites, who waited for others to tell them what to do; and particularly on the soldiers who fired only when they were commanded to, who moved only as and where they were ordered.

A little boy, deciding after reflection and with knowledge of what was involved, could choose a course of action and have this respected. When Standing Bear was eight, he decided to join the buffalo hunt on his own, as a hunter; until now, he had merely accompanied his father and grandfather. So he merely announced this decision to his family. When he was eleven, and met a recruiter for the Indian school at Carlisle which was about to open its doors, he announced to the White that he would join the school. It was a very courageous decision, and different from anything that the school authorities had in mind. Now that the warpath was forbidden by the White government, this opened to the Indian boy a wonderful opportunity for going bravely into enemy territory, and thus proving his mettle. But Standing Bear's decision was not accepted by the White recruiter; he would have no conclusive dealings with a little boy. He sent him to get his father. The father asked "Do you want to go?" The boy answered, "Yes." That was all.

In all this, the community does not protect itself against the autonomy of the individual. Somehow, just as individual dignity is taken for granted so is communal responsibility and concern; they are there, given. The infant experiences community as a dimension in many ways. His lullabies refer to him not in individualistic terms, but in terms of his significance to the community, not just as a hunter but a provider for the camp; not just as a warrior, but a defender. If he sees his father giving up a prized and loved possession, showing great autonomous strength, he sees him simultaneously, in the very same act, giving *to* someone in need; and the act of giving up itself celebrates the feat of another—it does not mark a personal achievement of the giver. For instance, when young Standing Bear announced his courageous decision to go to Carlisle, his father invited everyone who lived in the vicinity and gave to them all the goods in his trading store, honoring his son, sacrificing, and endowing the community in the same act. These were ordinary commonplace occurrences in the life of the Dakota. They took place in some form every day. And the growing child saw the socially responsible valued and honored, truly and consistently. Even the opportunity to take on responsibility for others was offered as an honor; as when a chief, upon a communal buffalo hunt, tapped special young men carefully chosen, and designated their day's hunt for the indigent. The men glowed with pride and honor.

Concern and caring for the community had to manifest themselves in behavior; a "feeling" of responsibility is not enough. And this behavior presupposed development of all aspects of the self. So, the strengthening of character, of courage, of the capacity to endure; the development of the powers of observation, of the ability to concentrate; the stretching of the span of attention, and everything that we subsume under the name of education, all this the individual undertook as part of his responsibility to community. Even infants had to learn not to cry at night for the sake of the camp, so as not to betray to lurking enemy scouts the whereabouts of the camp. (I have to believe this, since both Whites and Dakota assert that babies did learn not to cry at night.) "When a mere child," writes Standing Bear, "Father inspired me by often saying: 'Son, I never want to see you live to be an old man. Die young on the battle-field.' . . . The full intent of the advice was that I must never shirk my duty to my tribe no matter what price in sacrifice I paid."

The community could safely leave itself vulnerable to the autonomy of its members because these wanted to be responsible. These valued their responsibility; and thus the ends of the individual coincided with communal ends. Conversely, this desire to be responsible moved the individual to undertake the process of his own arduous education autonomously, without extraneous incentives. If he valued generosity, he had to go through the unimaginably demanding education required of the hunter and warrior; because to give, one has to give what he has acquired through his own skill and bravery. He may give horses which he has captured from the enemy at the risk of his life; or he may give the product of his hunting; and both these presuppose such detailed knowledge, such precise skills, such development of personal qualities as would take me much too long to list here.

The community was not just something which demanded unidirectional concern and responsibility. It was ever present in the individual in its supporting aspects. Standing Bear, for instance, talks about his first bow and arrows which his father gave him when he was old enough to walk alone. "He made them himself, painting the bow red, which signified that he had been wounded in battle (not just to catch the eye of the little boy). The arrows were likewise painted red. . . . That bow and arrows was the beginning of my Indian training. It was to be my weapon in war and was to get my food for me. . . . Some day, he said, he would like to see me go on the warpath and earn my own credits. So I kept my bow and arrows near me all the time as—can you guess the end of the sentence?—it told of my father's bravery of which I was very proud."

This intermixture of autonomy and community, then, is basic and so assured, that neither has to be on the watch against encroachment. It is from this unambiguous base that the individual starts on the path of development.

Take Charles Eastman, for instance, who at the time was known as Hakadah. When he was five or six, he took off in the early morning. No one sent him out, no one told him where to go, or what places to avoid; no one told him when to get back, or what to do if he got tired or bored. He wanted to go and he went; he chose to go now, so now he went. He was not killing time nor avoiding the boredom of home. This was his own choice. He did not have to ask permission, but this did not mean that his family did not care. His uncle, who was taking the place of father, said to him: "Look closely to everything you see." Only this. The boy went forth, perhaps joining friends, perhaps wandering all day alone. When he returned in the evening his uncle was there, waiting for him with questions. He was a busy man, a famous hunter, a great warrior. The busy man had time for the little boy; he cared.

So now the uncle asks questions; "On which side of the trees is the lighter colored bark?" The boy has not been told to look for this. But he has been admonished to look closely, and he has done so. He can answer. The uncle listens attentively and asks more questions. The boy describes the birds he has seen, their color, the shape of their bills, their song, the appearance and locality of their nest. He ventures a name; but this is only a guess. It is not for him to name; this depends on the language of the community. So the uncle corrects him and gives him the "proper" name. The whole process is autonomous—but what would it have been without the involvement of the uncle?

Eastman describes several occasions, when he is seven or eight, when he is helped to make his own observations the basis of conclusions and knowledge. There is the time when the boy realizes that to conclude that there are fish in the lake just because he saw them jumping out is an easy way out. He has to put his mind to work on the grouping of pebbles he observed, and the lines on the sandy bottom.

This, to me, is inviolate autonomy. I put it this way, because the fear of violation is always lurking in me. But the uncle has no such fear. After this last session, he proceeds to "violate" autonomy. He goes on and tells Hakadah: "The wolf . . . even when he is surprised and runs for his life . . . will pause and take one more look. . . ." He talks at length. The boy is not offended at being told instead of finding out for himself; and he listens with interest. Neither does this now seduce him from autonomous pursuit, leading him to seek the easy way of vicarious knowledge.

When I gave my definition of autonomy I spoke of the strong thrust which was needed in becoming engaged with experience. In the bringing up of the Dakota boy, I find community continually helping the individual to deal with the difficult, that from which he might have flinched. Hakadah tells of how he learned to deal with sudden fright without going to pieces, with temptation, with corroding fear. As long as he could remember, his uncle made a practice of awakening him in the morning with a war-whoop, and the little boy, perhaps four or five, had to learn "to leap up with perfect presence of mind." Sometimes he would challenge him to fast all day with him, and his little friends would tempt him with offers of food he had to refuse. There is no question of his learning not to be scared, not to be tempted; what he had to learn was to live through the forbidding experience.

A man from a neighboring tribe tells of being taught endurance. He had to learn it for himself, but the first task was set by his community: "When a boy got up in the morning his face was blacked with charcoal, and he was sent out to kill some game for food. It might be a quail, a rabbit, or a squirrel, seldom larger game than that. He was given no food until he returned with what he was sent out to procure. Because his face was blacked everyone who saw him knew why he was out, and no one gave him food or helped him in any way. Unaided he must find what he had gone out to kill. He was absolutely on his own resources. Sometimes it was found in a few minutes or a few hours. More often it took long hours of searching and wandering; just a matter of luck. It took me two days to kill the quail my father had sent me out to bring home. Quail was plentiful then, but I just could not kill one with my bow and arrow it seemed. After wandering for hours without food, my aim was not steady, and there is something in feeling that so much depends on one's efforts—that a test is being made. But at last my arrow brought one down, and I retraced my steps homeward.

"Oh, the joy, the pride that filled one's heart when he returned home victorious to a waiting and watchful family! An Indian boy automatically went on with his own training after such tests as I have described, encouraged and urged on by his father, his friends, and members of his social clan."

Community starts him; after this, he can proceed on his own. And in fact, even before, he was on his own. No one checked on him, no one saw that he did not take the quail from the kill of a friend, or that he kept his fast.

Standing Bear speaks of the time when all the braves go off after the Pawnee who have been reported on the hunting territory of his tribe, leaving the camp without fresh meat. His grandfather decides to go after buffalo, and takes the little seven-year-old boy with him. Standing Bear has been riding since he can remember, catching his own pony, and going off as he pleased. But on this occasion, when he is going off on this hazardous expedition, his grandfather saddles a horse for him. Soon they hear a thundering of hoofs, buffalo evidently frightened by the enemy. The grandfather leaves the boy behind the hill, terrified both of the buffalo and the Pawnee, simply telling him to remain where he was. The buffalo rush by, and presently the boy sees that his grandfather has killed a buffalo, and joins him. The little boy has been incredibly brave, living with his fear and staying with it, not betraying his whereabouts through "childish" acts. The grandfather makes no comment on this. He cuts a fine piece of tripe, adds to it a bit of marrow—all things that the little boy can do for himself—and hands it to his grandson. Apparently he is not afraid that with this pampering act he will destroy the child's pride.

By the time he is eight, Standing Bear decides that he can join the communal hunt. This means he knows the rules, he is ready to walk "in a sacred manner," he is ready to acquiesce to the strict structure of this occasion. And community, which accepts his decision has laid itself completely open to his fallibility; it is vulnerable to his possible "childishness." If he acts irresponsibly, for the heck of it, if he makes a mistake that scares the buffalo away, the entire community may have to go without buffalo meat for weeks.

He makes his announcement to his family. His father responds by making him a special bow and some steel-pointed arrows . . . "While one of my step-mothers was helping me (get ready) she said, 'Son, when you kill a buffalo, save me a kidney and the skin' . . . it made me proud to have her talk like that to me." His father talked to him "as if I were a man." He gives him advice. The boy goes off.

When finally the word goes that the hunters can go off on their own, Standing Bear starts out and soon finds himself "mixed up in the dust . . . All I could hear was the roar and rattle of the hoofs of the buffalo as they thundered along . . . I realized how small I was. I was really afraid of them. Then I thought of what my step-mother had said to me about bringing her a kidney and a skin, and the feeling that I was a man [he was eight] came back to me."

Here is community. The step-mother has not insisted that he make his own preparation; she does it for him, though I am sure he could have done it himself. At the same time, she believes in him, she is waiting for the kidney and the skin. His father is not afraid that he will harm or offend him if he does things for him, if he offers him the result of his own experience. He treats him as a man; and this is what Standing Bear carries with him; both the cherishing, and the belief in him. And he comes back with a buffalo, his first and last buffalo.

One more incident from the life of Standing Bear. Now he is ten. His father invites him to come on the warpath with him. "I felt real big and brave," says Standing Bear. His father makes over his own war-bonnet to fit over his son's head. Could not the boy have done this? Then, the third time they made camp, the father talks to the boy: "Son, I wanted you to come with me, because I wanted you to do something of great bravery or get killed on the battlefield. . . . I will take you as near as possible to the camp of the enemy the night before. . . . Ride through the camp as fast as your horse can run. I will be behind you, and if you pass through without harm . . . I will be proud of you. But if the enemy is ready to shoot you, as they nearly always are, and you fall in their midst, keep your courage . . . I will be with you my son." "I was willing to do my father's bidding," adds Standing Bear, "as I wanted so much to please him."

This is the boy's opportunity to earn his own credits, to prove himself a man, to himself and to his community. His father is not afraid to perform tender services for him. He sends him out on the hazardous mission. The son is "very happy" to know this, but just the same, it is the father's decision. The son does not initiate; he chooses to accept his father's decision. The father says to him, in effect, "This is your own life, and your own death, your voyage. Whether you win or lose, whether you fail and are in despair, you are on your own. That is the way I want you to die. I will not come in to save you. But I will be behind you, I will be with you." The boy is to go on, in utter autonomy, but he will not be alone; he carries his community with him.

Actually, the boy never did go into the midst of the enemy. And here comes another of the apparent paradoxes, apparent because they are only in my own mind, contradicting my own presuppositions. When they camped for the fourth time, an old chief overtook them, bringing to them the pipe of peace. If the proffered pipe of peace was not accepted, some great calamity would befall. The father accepts the pipe and they go home. He obeys. Brave and proud and autonomous as he is, he obeys when the occasion calls for obedience. The young people are turbulent; one young man even attempts to shoot the old chief to keep him from offering the pipe, which will put an end to the war-party. The little boy, greatly disappointed, is even ashamed, but not of his father; only because he has to turn back without seeing the enemy. Two men in the party do disobey the mandate of the pipe, and meet disaster. The father obeys with dignity. This does not diminish his autonomy, which remains as strong as ever.

I want to quote one more incident, this time from the life of Charles Eastman. He is eight, and this is the time for him to take the first step toward establishing a relation with Wakan Tanka, the Great Mystery. Later on, he will proceed on his own, at his chosen time. But at this time, he has to learn, and community has to teach him. Besides, the first step is indescribably difficult. He needs to be held to the experience, lest he flinches away from it in pain and horror. Now he has to make the first true, agonizing sacrifice to his God. Later, he will sacrifice his own flesh, at his own initiative, at his own will, at the appalling and glorious occasion of the sundance. But first he has to learn the meaning of sacrifice, and he has to learn the wrench and joy of sacrifice.

This day Hakadah has been hunting with his dog who shares his life and helps him in all his activities. When he comes back, his grandmother who is taking the place of his dead mother, is waiting for him. She tells him that this is the day for his first sacrifice—she does not leave it up to him to decide; she informs him. The boy is delighted. He knows that only in a relation with his God can he grow into a true man, a true Dakota, effective in the hunt, in war, in his relation to his community and to the universe. And the "relation" to the Great Mystery is not actual. It is there for him as a right to proceed along an open road; he will have to do the proceeding, to actualize the relation.

So he is proud that now he can begin on the road which his father, his uncle, his grandfather, and many other heroes have followed. He offers to give anything that his grandmother considers adequate; his best bow and arrows? his paints? his bear's claw necklace? The grandmother is not satisfied with any of these. She reminds him of the greatness of the Mystery of Mysteries; she tells him of the significance of the first offering. Hakadah, in an access of manliness offers to give anything that the grandmother suggests; and she points to the one possibility he has not thought of, because it is not a possibility for him: his dog. Eventually, the boy is convinced that this will be an honorable journey for his dog, to go as a messenger to the Great Mystery; but the pain of the loss is piercing.

Now he is left alone in the teepee and, at his own desire, he prepares his dog in the accoutrements of a hunter, fastening on him a wing from the oriole and the tails of the two squirrels that the dog has helped him kill; painting him with the paints of a man preparing himself for death. Then he goes further. He mixes ground coal and bear oil, and paints his [own] face black. Now with his hair loosened, he is in mourning for his dead friend—perhaps finding some comfort from the stab of pain.

But when he goes out, his grandmother will not allow him this small comfort, this small evasion. If he makes an offering, he must offer it with a will, not with regret. A mourned gift is not a gift. The boy has to go firmly through the unbearable experience, without padding.

As he recalls this, many years after, all that Eastman remembers is his grandmother's great love. He speaks of how, when he was preparing his dog to meet his death, his grandmother was watching him through a peephole in the tent wall; of how strongly she was tempted to spare him this anguish, how she struggled "with the storm and burden of her soul."

From now on, when the boy has handed his dog to the executioner, he has no more intolerable demands presented to him. Another puts the dog to death, another brings the body and places it on the ground, the grandmother performs the final ceremonies.

But the act of sacrifice, once it is recognized and accepted by the boy, is his own, in all its pain and unrelieved sharpness. And to meet this, to live through this, the boy has the firm guidance and undeviating hold of the loving grandmother.

This is the society in which I find autonomy and community in transaction. There is no "and" between them. I am forced to add it by my language, and also because I feel the need to join what my culture phrases as two isolates.

In this society autonomy remains clear and uncontaminated, strong and sure, so that there is no need to arm against community. Where there is such assurance, and such trust, obedience itself can be an autonomous act, a choosing to submit to the command of the trusted and valued. To see someone as a model, as having a clearer picture of the situation than I have, a better basis for making the decision, is no threat to my individuality. Where to develop, sensitize and discipline oneself, to educate oneself, is to enrich and strengthen the community, and is achieved with the caring involvement and support of the community, to speak of the cold war, of the strategy of techniques and planned consistency, is an absurdity.

BIBLIOGRAPHY

Black Elk Speaks, Being the Life History of a Holy Man of the Oglala Sioux, as told to John G. Neilhardt. New York: William Morrow and Company, 1932.

BROWN, JOSEPH EPES. *The Sacred Pipe, Black Elk's Account of the Seven Rites of the Oglala Sioux*. Recorded and edited by J. E. Brown. Norman: University of Oklahoma, 1953.

EASTMAN, CHARLES A. (Ohiyesa) *Indian Boyhood*. Boston: Little, Brown and Company, 1902.

NEILHARDT, JOHN G. *When the Tree Flowered; an Authentic Tale of the Old Sioux World*. New York: Macmillan Company, 1951.

STANDING BEAR, LUTHER. *My People the Sioux*. Boston: Houghton Mifflin Company, 1928.

———. *Land of the Spotted Eagle*. Boston: Houghton Mifflin Company, 1932.

WHAT PRICE LITERACY?

I gave the title of my talk as "What Price Literacy?" and I really meant it to be a question. I meant it to be the question Are we paying a heavy price for literacy? Are we giving up our heritage of wonder, of curiosity, of questing, of plunging into chaos and creating life out of it? Are we giving up our sense of mystery, the excitement of being lost in ambiguity and building a world out of it? Have we given up this heritage for the sake of literacy, which gives us a label instead of experience? This is not a rhetorical question; I asked the question and now I'm going to answer it, and I'm going to say we don't have to give up this heritage. I'm not sure that we are not doing it, but I think we don't have to. We are, however, I think living in an age where, in some way or another, we seem to have abdicated our right to be completely human, to experience, to think for ourselves, to choose, to feel for ourselves; and one way in which we have done this is in the fact that we often substitute literacy, the book, the sentence, the authoritative statement for our own authentic experience.

This is what I mean. You go to see a movie; you come out; somebody asks you about it. If you haven't read a review of it, quite often you are not sure whether you should be enthusiastic or not enthusiastic. The review tells you; and in a sense your own experience has not merit, or you do not accord it the worth, the value, the authenticity which is its own right just because you have

"What Price Literacy?" This is a slightly revised version of a talk given by Dorothy Lee at Claremont College Reading Conference, Claremont, Calif., in 1966.

been intimidated (and I say this about myself too; I have been intimidated by the written word or by the spoken word of authority).

I would say that literacy itself is neither good nor bad. I would say that it has potentials for wonderfully enriching my life; but it is good or bad only insofar as I address myself to it as a full human being, asking it to help me in my quest, or, conversely, if I do not address myself to it at all but simply let it take over instead of me, substituting it for me.

Some years ago, oh, many years ago, during the Second World War, a committee of scientists was called together over a weekend in Washington to discuss the very pressing problem of fatigue. They were very high-powered professors and others—physicists, biologists, etc.—and they sat together all day and way into the night for two days discussing fatigue and trying to come to a definition of "fatigue." At the end of the second day, close to midnight, they had not reached a definition but they decided to stop; and finally one man got up, stretched himself, and said, "Wow, I'm tired." It is not necessary to define fatigue.

Now there are people who are very much concerned right now over this aspect of our present-day culture, over our readiness to give up our autonomy in our life and our experience. Some years ago the psychiatrist Ernest Schachtel published a paper called "Memory and Childhood Amnesia" in which he said that we do not remember what happened to us as children before we were two or three because we had no words to name our experiences. By the time we are three or four we have gotten words for concepts and experiences; and from then on we do not remember the experience, we remember the words, we remember the name. What he was saying is that our experience has been replaced by labels; our memory consists of labels, not of experience. Now he was not talking of literacy. He was talking of words, he was talking of names, he was talking of substituting the word *fatigue* for the experience of being tired. I don't agree with him. I must say I do not feel so strongly against the word. I feel that the word can be evocative. I feel that when I say "water," for example, I need not see w-a-t-e-r or the sound of the word *water*. It can evoke for me the quenching of my thirst when I'm very, very thirsty; it can evoke the wonderful sensation of coolness in the hot summer; it can evoke the sound of a waterfall. It doesn't have to substitute for the experience; but I have to see to it that I'm not lazy and that I do not let it substitute for the experience. I think we do have to be vigilant, alert, ready for effort, because it is so much easier not to feel, to adopt the label. As I said, I think we're living in an era in which we have abdicated our human autonomy or human effort and have let something else take over. It may be literacy; it may be the word; it may be the machine; whatever it may be.

We have done it in a number of ways. For instance, Korzybski wrote of the map and the territory. He said that we must not confuse the map with the territory and the map can never substitute for the territory. The map, however (I can't remember whether he went on like this, but I'm going on like this), can enable me. It need not substitute for the territory. I don't fool myself when I look at the map that I've really been in Thailand. However, the map can excite me, can get me interested, can start me out, can tell me where to go, how to go, can have me look at the wonderfully exciting name and try to find out what lies behind this name. The map can enable me to search for or express what is important for me.

The map can, however, fool me and substitute for the territory. And, you know, I may fall to this temptation because the territory is pretty hard. Covering the territory means that I have to sweat, I have to go over rocks, I have to be bitten by insects, and get scratched by bushes. The map is easy; I can just sit and look at it, and quite often again I am tempted to do this.

I have been speaking in metaphor, but now I want to come back to the map itself, not the metaphor, and I want to repeat an experience that an African tells in an autobiography. This is an African who grew up in a tribal village and then went to school in Konakry. His father has been a trader, a kind of peddler carrying great bundles on his back and traveling great distances along the Niger; so when the son was away in school he thought how nice it would be to get a map of the territory of the Niger and bring it back to his father, and he did. He called his father and laid out the map and started showing his father the trips he had followed; and his father got more and more angry and finally burst out and said, "This isn't my journey. My journey is not on this line; my journey is in the pain of my muscles; my journey is in the joy of finally coming home. It is not on this piece of paper. Maps are liars," he said. "The things that hurt one do not show on a map. The truth of a place is in the joy and the hurt that come from it." The son saw that the journey was in the muscles, the heavy cargo on trek-weary feet. Yet this need not deny the map. Once you have the experience, once you know what it means to go through the territory, it can help you get a different view, perhaps a broader view, perhaps a more engaging view of what you have already experienced as a person.

Now this is, as I said, part of our attitude in our everyday affairs. It is not only to be seen in terms of literacy; but just as I can relate myself to the territory with my muscles, with my whole being, with all my senses, in the same way I can address myself to the written word without allowing it to substitute for me.

Louis H. Sullivan, architect, tells about the time he first went to school. He went to a one-room schoolhouse; he went to live on the farm of his grandparents so as to go to a little school near Boston in what is now greater Boston. He went to school; he was five; and he would listen to the lessons of everyone. He tells of how he would listen to arithmetic. The teacher would read out a problem, such as: if it takes four men to build three perches of wall in three days, how many days will two men take to do the same job? Louis would listen to this; he would see people, he would see a wall, and then he would say to himself: "Where is the wall to be built? For whom is it to be built? What is his name? What are the names of the men who are building the wall?" (for it was becoming a real wall). "Are they Irish or Scotch? Where did they get the stone to build the wall? Did they get it from the rough quarry across the road from the schoolhouse? Did they gather up boulders from the fields? Isn't this matter of four men and two men irrelevant?" Here was the boy not stopped by the slickness of literacy but seeing beyond the numbers, the wall, into all that was behind them, beyond literacy. The story, however, doesn't end here. There's a sequel to it. One day a letter came from the teacher to the grandfather to the effect that he was a dullard, he just could not pay attention, he was incapable of studying. Of course, he was not staying with the written word, he was going beyond it. He grew up to be a great architect and to be the teacher of Frank Lloyd Wright.

In the last hundred years or even more our writers have been concerned with this question of how to have the writing not simply tell me something so that I automatically receive it because it's written, but how to evoke me to create. If you think back this is true of the people that are difficult to read: Virginia Woolf, for instance, says in *The Second Common Reader*, "I want to make the reader my accomplice. I write in such a way as to evoke an answering experience in the reader so that what I say will not be simply a label but will be unfinished and the reader himself will work to finish it."

We have a number of societies. I can think now of societies in

Africa where the teaching of the child again is in this way. There also the explicit word is not used to substitute for the thinking, the involvement of the child, but is used to evoke what I call the *synergy* of the child. For instance, this is an area where proverbs are used in this sense all the time, not only with children but with adults. Among the Ngoni in East Africa, for instance, if a bunch of children are together and one of them starts bragging, one of the adults will throw a proverb in the air. Suddenly all the children will hear this proverb, which has something to do with a bird with a proud beak or something of the sort. The children will stop, will listen to the proverb, will translate it into what it really means; then each of them will say "Does this apply to me?" and eventually the braggart will stop. In a situation like that, in the communication between person and person, the word is not a label explicitly telling anyone, but the word is there to open up a further experience and to evoke thinking, judging, considering, and, finally, deciding on the part of the hearers.

Now I have started talking about preliterate, or rather nonliterate, groups, and I want to speak a little more at length about one nonliterate group that I have studied: the Dakota Indians in this country. I chose them—I don't know whether I should say the words "I chose them." I simply found these people who produced quite a number of autobiographies, people who were born about 1860 and either dictated or wrote their autobiographies, and I fall back on these people because they give me the material that I need for what I'm going to say.

I want to talk particularly about the life, the growing up and the education of Ohiyesa, otherwise known as Charles Eastman, a Dakota boy who grew up to go to the East and study medicine and become a doctor among his people. He was brought up by his grandmother and his uncle from the time he was a little boy of four; his family fled to Canada, fled from the Whites, his mother was dead, his father had been taken prisoner and the family thought he had been killed. He tells about how he became educated. In the morning—when he was five, six, or seven—at daybreak, he would emerge from the tepee. His uncle was there; all that his uncle would say to him was, "Look carefully at everything you see." Nobody sent the boy out, the boy went; nobody told him where to go, how long to go, when to come back. Nobody suggested what he should look at. He simply went. He would come back in the afternoon. His uncle, who was a great warrior and a famous hunter, was home to receive him and they would have a conversation, perhaps for an hour. The boy would report where he had gone. The uncle would say "On which side of the trees does the bark grow the thicker?" and the boy would answer. The boy had not been told to go to the forest. The boy had not been told to look at the trees, to look at the bark. He had simply been told to look carefully, and the boy addressed himself with his own questions and answered them, so that when he came back to his uncle he could answer whatever questions his uncle asked. Now this boy did not go out with any labels. He created his world out of his own experience. In a recent autobiography of childhood, the author talks about his own childhood and says "Nothing more resembles God's eyes than the eyes of a child." They see the world for the first time and create it. Before this the world was chaos. The Dakota Indians proceeded on this principle, I think, and the children went out into chaos and created the world for themselves. The little boy of five, six or seven would come back, having looked, and, with the help of the questions of his uncle, would create his world; but he had looked with a questing eye already.

Ohiyesa talks further about how he learned to categorize. There was a little cousin living with him, and he tells about the time when he and his cousin were there with the grandmother and started having a discussion about a lizard. The little boy said that the lizard belonged to the walking tribe. The little girl said that the lizard belonged to the creeping tribe. So they turned to the grandmother. The grandmother did not give them an answer. Instead she suggested that the children go out and catch a lizard. They came home, smoothed the floor of the tepee and sprinkled some fine dirt on it; they put the lizard down; the lizard ran across and they looked. There were indeed footmarks all along, but in the middle there was also a line where the lizard had dragged its tummy. So then they turned to the grandmother. At this point, you see, the children had gone with curiosity, had done their own research. The one thing that they did not have was the tribal definition of the words "creeping" tribe and "walking" tribe; they did not have the labels. For this they turned to authority. They turned to the grandmother. The grandmother said for an animal to be delegated to the category of walking there must be no dragging at all, no touching of the body on the ground. So now the children, again having, let's say, looked up the definition of the tribe by themselves, decided to which category the lizard belonged. The grandmother at this time did not tell them the lizard belonged to the creeping tribe; she only gave them the definition.

These are nonliterate people bringing up their children in such a way that at every point they go from experience to the label, from experience to the category, from data to conclusions but not vice versa. Of course, you will say this is something that people who live in nature can do very easily, or you might say that this is something people can do who have lots of time. I want to say that the grandmother didn't have that much time either. She had to build her own house, that is to make her own tepee, she had to go and find her own herbs for her own medicine, she had to cut up the buffalo that her son brought, she had to work from morning till night, but she had time to give no quick answer to the children but rather lead them so that they would discover the world through their own mind, their own senses, their own powers of judgment and concluding. She had time so as not to substitute the label for the experience.

I would also like to say, however, that we have societies which are literate where again the individual is brought up and trained in such a way that he relates himself to the book with the same kind of questing, the same kind of reluctance to take the book as the finished answer, the same urge to explore question and experience. Some years ago I spent some time studying the education of the Jews in Eastern Europe, the Jews who lived in the small type communities, the *shtetl*, which, as you know, were destroyed during the Second World War. In this the children, once they were taught how to read, not how to write, how to read and how to understand Hebrew, were encouraged in every way never to accept any authoritative statement whether it was verbal or written. If a bearded scholar made a statement, a little boy of eight, nine, ten would be expected to and encouraged to question and he would be encouraged to uphold his own objection, his own questioning, his own comment, until eventually perhaps he could maintain his own stand alongside the stand of the famous scholar. The scholar, conversely, would recognize the right of the boy to question, and by respecting him and answering back, not with condescension or kindness in his voice or delight, let's say, of how well the little boy talked or something like that, but in treating him as another scholar he encouraged the boy to question any statement before finally he might even agree to it and say, "Yes, this is what I would like also to state." In the schools, the boys (and only boys were going to school) were given what might have seemed, to me at any rate, very dreary things to read—commentaries on the Torah, on one of the books of the Old Testament, for example. However, apparently, the boys addressed themselves to these with delight, with vigor, because at every point they were asked to come up with new questions, some new interpretation of a passage that had been interpreted by thousands of people. The boy was encouraged and invited to use his imagination, his ingenuity, his questing, until finally he found just one point that had not been questioned before.

Now these young people had a very, what seems to me very, narrow area within which they could be creative, within which they could explore through their own particular ingenuity, and this, in itself, was challenging, so that they would come forth with the most minute, refined and apparently exciting questions—questions addressed to literacy, to a verse that had been read and expounded for hundreds of years. So I believe that if we can address ourselves with openness to the matter of experience, with openness and energy, with effort, and not be afraid to think for ourselves, not be afraid to state our authentic conclusion and not too lazy to exert ourselves, we do not have to say that literacy substitutes for experience. I say this knowing that millions of people have been brought up by their parents, have gone to school, in such a way that they don't even know that there is experience behind the words that they use. I myself deal with many students like this at the college level or the graduate level who will throw these wonderful, big words at me, who will write papers composed of nothing but words which have nothing behind them—what we call clichés, what Shakespeare called "abjects, orts, and imitations." These are words that are not the name of a thought on the part of the student but are words strung together. I make it my business to take up every one of these words and ask the student "What do you mean by this word?" The answer usually is a sentence composed of more words which don't mean anything at all. It's just substituting one set of words for another. After that I have to work with great pain and suffering, and my students with more pain and suffering, until finally they can smash through this kind of granite covering and recognize the fact that there is existence, thinking, experience, suffering, sensing behind this innocuous little word. I think I'm going to stop here, because I'm hoping that possibly you will not take my words as labels and will question me and bring in your own experience.

DEVELOPING THE POTENTIAL TO LEARN

As an anthropologist, I am concerned with the cultural factors which may inhibit or encourage the development of the potential to learn. Such factors reach the individual through the society of which he is a member, through the family and community, on the one hand, and, on the other, directly through the school.

Cultural factors are built into the experience presented to the growing child; and their strength lies in this. For instance, if a school does not value effort particularly, a low demand for effort is built into the curriculum itself. Even if it does value effort, it may find itself in conflict with a community which does not. The child will read the advertisement of an electrical vibrator, for instance, which urges its readers to "exercise without effort." All around him, he will see technology used to spare people from putting forth effort—from bending, walking, lifting; from exerting their minds to calculate, and from exertion in general.

I have chosen this instance advisedly because for me *development* and *develop* are active words, active concepts. To develop, I have to engage myself in the experience, exercising my capacities and exercising them with effort. So I have posed to myself the question: What are the factors which motivate the individual to develop his capacity to learn?

"Developing the Potential to Learn," by Dorothy Lee. Original title "Developing the Drive to Learn and the Questioning Mind." From Alexander Frazier, ed., *Freeing Capacity to Learn* (Washington, D.C.: Association for Supervision and Curriculum Development, 1960), pp. 10-22. Copyright © 1960 by the Association for Supervision and Curriculum Development. Reprinted by permission of the publisher. A paper read at the Association for Supervision and Curriculum Development Institute, May 2, 1959, at Los Angeles.

This question has apparently concerned the Western world from ancient times. Plutarch suggested that the growing boy be "led" and "urged" to excellence through admonition and reasoning, praise and blame, but "not, in heaven's name, blows and torments." St. Augustine described an education which was enforced by punishment. And reflecting on how he hated Greek which he had learned through being "urged vehemently with cruel threats and punishments," on how he loved the study of Latin, which he learned "without pressure of punishment . . . for my heart urged me to give birth to its conceptions," he concluded that "a free curiosity has more force in our learning these things than a frightful enforcement."

Saint Augustine's description of his own education, however, raises a question which will concern me in this paper. He says that learning to read and write was a "burden and penalty"; that "one and one, two; two and two, four" was "a hateful sing-song"; that he was beaten because he played ball instead of studying. Yet he did learn the hated Greek; he did learn reading and writing and arithmetic, and if he hated them, the hatred was overcome. There is no doubt that he went on studying eagerly, going on his own initiative much further than he was required to, or expected to. All this "frightful enforcement" did not interfere with the development of his capacity to learn; if it did not motivate him, neither did it stop him. It did not make him hate all learning, all intellectual development; perhaps because in itself it did not have the power to stop growth, or because there was a powerful motivation which nothing could stop.

It is with such a powerful motivation that I concern myself here—with the cultural factors and particularly the factor of values which incite the individual to develop his potential to the utmost. I have purposely chosen to speak of societies where the motivation is strong, spurring the individual to put forth all he has. Such a motivation sweeps away all that might have been interferences under different circumstances. In my study of other societies, I have been impressed by the fact that education takes place under conditions which we would regard as totally unfavorable to learning, and in fact would see as obstructing the growth of the spirit of inquiry, or the desire to learn. Yet in these societies I have found that the people in general continue developing their potential to learn, working at this on their own initiative, pursuing their education until death. Conversely, when the motivating force is lacking, no amount of removal of "interferences" seems to bring about a strong development of the individual's capacities to learn.

In my study, I have found children consistently learning to read before, according to our notions, they can be biologically ready; and showing the ability to concentrate before they can possibly have a long enough attention span. I have found originality valued and exercised where learning was acquired by imitation and repetition with hard discipline and a multitude of regulations. In China, for instance, the learning of painting came after the mastery of calligraphy, which was taught through prolonged tracing and copying, under conditions of rigorous discipline. The Tao of painting itself includes an immense number of minutely detailed regulations. All this would seem to spell a devaluation of the free spirit, of individuality. Yet this is exactly what was valued. A painter-monk wrote: "I am always myself and must be present in my work. . . . The lungs and bowels of the old masters cannot be transformed into my stomach. I express my own lungs and bowels and show my own beard and eyebrows." When a value is present and strong, no obstacle, I believe, can stop its expression. If an obstacle does act as an interference, this is because the value is weak, or not truly present.

To show how cultural factors support the development of capacity, as expressed in the community as well as through the curriculum and the methods of teaching, I shall speak of two societies [which we looked at in earlier chapters]. I shall speak briefly of a nonliterate society, the Oglala Sioux of the Dakotas, and at greater length of a highly literate society, the Jewish *shtetl* of Eastern Europe, the tight Jewish communities to be found in small towns or villages.

Among the Oglala Sioux, a child, and particularly a boy, was brought up from infancy on to be aware of his responsibility for the camp circle, and, as he learned eventually, for the entire universe. To carry out this responsibility, the individual had to develop all his capacities to the utmost. This was conveyed to the growing child so that the exercise of his potential became something to be undertaken on his own initiative. Children would seek out competitive situations, so that they could be challenged to strain beyond their limits of exertion and hardihood.

The responsibility of the Oglala individual reflected the significance of the individual within the world order. On the one hand, a man had to be worthy of the friendship and aid of the animals and plants to whom he was related. On the other hand, the Great Spirit needed man's work for the actualization of his design; and man had to develop all his capacities fully, to be able to carry out this tremendously significant task. So hardihood, keen perception and sensitivity, precision of skill, knowledge of ceremonials, the ability to draw valid conclusions and form sound judgments, were all demanded for the significant role of the individual; and they were so strongly supported by the cultural values that exertion and capacity to stand and enjoy hardship were in themselves highly valued.

The education of the child emphasized the full development of capacity. From infancy on, they were taught to use their senses to the utmost, to sit still and listen to that which they could not hear, to smell and see and become aware of that which was not obvious to the senses. In addition, they were taught to engage themselves in the elements—to meet them with an answering strength. If a torrential rain fell, they learned to strip and run out in it, however cold the weather. Little boys were trained to walk with the men for miles through heavy snowdrifts in the face of biting winds, and to take pride in the hardship endured. In the winter, they broke the ice on the water to plunge in for their bath. Step by step, the Sioux boy learned to endure incredible hardship, to face great danger, and to court it in the face of his fear.

The effort to exercise one's potential to its fullest was encouraged by the tremendous emphasis on the personal, the individual. Everyone had a right to his own private, unfiltered experience. According to one Oglala writer, as we saw earlier, a mother would take her baby out and attract his attention to different animals and birds long before he talked; and only after he had learned to notice them unlabeled, did she name them for him. Later, the children were sent out to observe, and then, through discussion, were helped to arrive at conclusions on the basis of their observation. Children had to learn to act on their own initiative, to come to their own decisions, which were then respected by the group. The potential was recognized; and children had to learn to put forth effort, to engage themselves in experience by way of exercising and developing potential. Man was potentially related to the Great Spirit; but even here, he could establish this relationship only through his own tremendous effort. Nothing was made easy for the learning child; and those Oglala who later recorded their autobiographies remember that they gloried in doing the difficult; they found a challenge in being faced by that which was beyond their immediate ability.

The next group I shall speak about, the *shtetl* Jews of Eastern Europe were urban and literate; yet, in the factors influencing the capacity to learn, their culture exhibits certain similarities to that of the nonliterate Oglala. Among these, too, the individual is called to tremendous effort in developing his capacity to learn, or to aid learning. The great emphasis on originality, on individuality, is here also. And, as with the Oglala, education, the pursuit of learning, ideally ends only at death.

In these Jewish communities, education was the duty and privilege of all because through education man could perform his duty to God and carry out his responsibility to the community. And here, too, there was a love of learning; and, as in the case of the Oglala, the tremendous effort involved in the pursuit of learning is a remembered joy in the autobiographies.

In the culture of the Eastern European Jews, the strong value supporting the pursuit of learning was absolutely necessary if there was to be education at all, because, according to our theories, everything was wrong with the educational system—the children went to school long before their eyes could focus properly on the tiny marks on the page; they were offered an uninteresting curriculum in a strange language; the teaching was pedagogically unsound, the teachers lacked compassion and understanding; the days were too long, the schoolrooms unpleasant.

Only boys were sent to school; and they were practically torn from their mothers' arms at infancy. It was not unusual to start school at three, and usually boys started before five. The *kheder*, to which the little boy went, is described as "crowded, noisy and unventilated," small and ill-lit; a room with a long table flanked by hard, backless benches on which the little boys sat for ten hours a day, five and a half days a week.

The first books for the little student were prayer-books, in ordinary print, without pictures to attract the child's attention. Through these, he had to learn the letters and then the words of an unknown tongue—Hebrew—and later to memorize each word through endless mechanical repetition. Only later was he given the meaning, which he also had to memorize; and eventually he learned to understand the meaning of a sentence. But at this time, no attempt was made to help the boy to understand the meaning of the whole.

In a few months, as soon as he had mastered the mechanics of reading, he was graduated to the *Pentateuch*. This was full of interesting stories, but not for the little four-year-old. He had to learn to master the ritualistic detail of the *Leviticus*.

There were few diversions in the ten-hour school day. In the afternoon, the teacher went to the synagogue for about an hour, and the children were free to play, perhaps even outside in the school yard. Sometimes the children went home after nine hours, and came back for a two-hour session at night. And there was a break for lunch, when the poorer children ate their piece of bread dry, while the others might buy syrup to dip their bread in, or hot soup from a peddler. There were no educational games to help the child learn and "relieve the tedium." The children did not even have pencil and paper to play with. Writing was not a part of the curriculum, playing was not considered necessary, and, in addition, many of the children could not afford to buy paper and pencils. Besides, it would be a distraction; and the child had to learn to pay unwavering attention. If his attention wandered, if he was not ready to pronounce the word at which the teacher's stick pointed, he was usually severely punished.

To this school the children often went barefoot, out of poverty. They had to take their own candles to school for the hours of dark, and a lantern to light their way back through the unlighted streets. And there were not always enough books to be shared among the children, though none of the reports I know mention the extremity that was found among the Jews of Yemen, many of whose children, when they arrived in Palestine, could read only upside down, since they had sat across the table from the teacher who held the only book in the *kheder.*

Perhaps all this would not have mattered if the teacher was filled with enthusiasm for learning, with the love of teaching, with tenderness and understanding for the little boys who were struggling through this difficult curriculum. But in most cases, the teachers in these schools are described as ignorant, miserable, unjust, cruel to the children. Sholem Aleichem reports that whippings were so usual in his school that there was no feeling of shame attached to them; the resulting sores were painful, but the boys said, "They'll heal before we are married." The teacher is generally described as having taken up teaching through default, "fallen into his profession because he failed elsewhere."

Yet out of this miserable schoolroom came people whose one desire was to be scholars for life; who, when the path of secular studies was open to them became great philosophers or teachers or men of letters or scientists. Not only in adulthood, but even in childhood we find this burning, self-directed application to study. A Lithuanian Jew tells how, at the age of nine, he left home and moved in with a teacher, since the only time this man could give him instruction in the Talmud was at 5:00 A.M. After two years, he and a friend decided that they could get better instruction in another town, and they went there, without even consulting their parents. A gunny-sack filled with straw and laid on a bench in the synagogue made an adequate bed; and meals were probably provided by the different households in the Jewish community, which usually undertook to feed the students who came from elsewhere. These were small boys of eleven, acting on their own initiative.

Morris Cohen, who is remembered by many as a brilliant professor of philosophy in New York, also speaks of such initiative in pursuit of learning at an early age. His education had been Talmudic; so when, at eleven, he found someone who had a manuscript on arithmetic, he copied this by hand for his own use. At this time also, he discovered books on history and the history of civilization which could be had for rent; and, on his own initiative, he started a small business which netted enough money to pay the rent on such secular books. I am mentioning here only a few of the many instances I have found reported which show the readiness for total involvement, total effort in developing the potential to learn.

How did this love of learning, this personal search for knowledge, survive the miserable schoolroom? I asked a student of mine, a Besarabian Jew who had gone to school at the age of three under conditions which I found appalling. I said, "Were you very miserable?" He answered, "Miserable? I was learning the language of the ritual; I was learning to say the chants like my father and my older brother. I was proud." And this statement, with variations, is repeated in many of the reports. Ideally, much of the father's time was spent at home over his sacred books. Even if he did not devote all his time to study, he studied in the morning before he went to work, or in the evening; or at least he would devote the Sabbath to study. Perhaps the only time that the father paid attention to his little boy was over this subject of studying; as he read the sacred books, he would often take the baby boy on his lap, swaying with him as he chanted, pointing out reverently the black marks on the pages. When the boy learned to read and understand Hebrew, he was initiated into this, his father's world. It was actually his initiation into male adulthood. When, at the end of a year or so of schooling, he passed, amidst great celebration, the examination showing that he had mastered the mechanics of reading, he received recognition from his father; and all the community accorded him the first marks of the kind of respect accorded to adult men.

So learning to read Hebrew, to the little boy, meant identifying himself with his father and the valued male role; it meant the awakening of respect from others, and a recognition of his status as a male. As he grew older, he found out that the value of learning went beyond that. To study meant to obey the command of God; and only through studying the Scripture could one be a good Jew.

From early babyhood, the child was exposed to the value of learning. The mother lulling her baby, sang of her hopes of scholarship for the boy, and of a scholarly bridegroom for the girl. A baby's hairline was sometimes shaved back to give him the appearance of intellectuality. When a four or five year old was ready to take his first examination to prove his ability to read, this was an occasion of tremendous importance for family, relatives, friends. And, after this, when he was introduced to the study of the commentary of Rashi, his father, as well as visiting scholars would engage the little boy seriously in learned argument. Later, a bearded man might bring a difficult Talmudic question to a boy of thirteen. So learning, on the one hand, was presented as of infinite value; and on the other hand, it earned, not condescending praise, but true respect, a welcoming acceptance into the fellowship of men.

The value of education was manifested in another way. All boys, except perhaps orphans with no relatives, went to school, though education was neither compulsory nor free; the school-teacher had to be paid a fee for each child. And this tuition fee was the most important item in the budget. Food costs would be cut, jewelry pawned to raise the fee. Morris Cohen speaks of how his mother, who at the time was supporting a number of children with her peddling, could yet manage to raise enough to engage a teacher to teach him to write, since this was not a part of the school curriculum for which she was also paying a fee. At this time, young Morris was going to school barefoot, and was practicing writing with his finger or a stick, on sand, since there was no money for writing materials. The people of his village "wore rags on their feet and ate white bread only on the Sabbath, but no child went without schooling."

A learned man was a valued man, was the pride of the community; he had authority and status. He was a *sheyne* Jew, a "beautiful" Jew, and able to sit closest to the east wall of the synagogue, the place of highest honor. There were in the community the few manual workers who, as unfortunate orphans, had no one to pay their school fees, and were doomed to a low status; but many of the manual workers did have some basic learning so that they could at least spend the Sabbath in the synagogue pursuing their studies. And there were those who spent much of their time in business, who were well-to-do and who considered it a privilege to endow a daughter with a large dowry so that they could acquire a learned son-in-law, and to support him in his further studies; or to give money to a *yeshiva,* a school of higher learning. There were the women, whose highest function was to enable men to continue their scholarship; many wives earned the livelihood for the family while their husbands devoted themselves to their studies. And there were the people of small means who, if they lived in a town which had a school of Talmudic studies, invited the students to as many meals a week as they could afford.

George Spindler uses the term *cultural compression* to describe just this kind of situation in which only one alternative is possible without self-degradation. The little Jewish boy saw only one way open to him—excellence in scholarship; and, if not in scholarship, then excellence in business dealings which would make such scholarship possible for others. Mediocrity, noninvolvement, effort-less existence were not alternatives unless one was ready to cease to be a true and good Jew.

It is this consistence and clarity of value in the culture, ramified through the myriad details of living, which, to my mind, sustained the little boy through the dreadfully difficult first years of his schooling, so that he achieved what appears a superhuman task, and came out of the experience without learning to hate all learning. And this value sustained him through life. But in itself it is not enough to account for the *kind* of scholarship we find among the Jews, for the inquiring spirit, the incisive, challenging mind which enabled a man to pursue his Talmudic studies throughout his life, attacking the book with fresh vigor and inquiry every time he started a new reading of it, making an original interpretation which he was able to defend against all opposition. What accounts for this, I believe, is the emphasis on individual difference, individual creativity, which was expressed in the kind of education a boy had after he left the primary school I have been describing, an education supported and echoed in the home and the attitudes of the community.

In the earliest school, for the first few months, the child had merely been mastering the mechanics of reading through repetition and memorization, without understanding. At the next stage, he learned to translate. Now, as he read the Pentateuch, he was also given a commentary to read and study, so that he could become acquainted with the search for hidden meanings, and the value of individual interpretation. From now on, and particularly when he was graduated to the study of the Talmud, the entire emphasis was placed on the searching for oneself, on the exercise of individual imagination, on the making of an original synthesis, on the raising of questions which were peculiarly one's own; and, above all, on never accepting a statement without a search for its assumptions and implications—not even the statement of a rabbi, or of the Torah.

Even in the earliest school, individuality had been given some recognition; each child read aloud at his own rhythm, pitching his chant at his own individual level. But it was in the Talmudic studies that this autonomy of opinion was given full scope. The students were encouraged to compare different interpretations, analyze all possible facets of each, weigh opposing opinions, and finally to come through with a unique solution. To do this, the student must be involved at his fullest, drawing on memory and imagination, on logic and wit, attacking every statement the teacher makes, arguing with subtlety and incisiveness. An eye-witness describes students pressing against the teacher's platform, shouting contradictions, challenging every sentence. "This mental activity combines the pleasures and satisfactions of high scholarship and of high spirit," writes Zborowski, who grew up in a *shtetl*. The teacher himself enjoyed and encouraged these vociferous attacks.

This individuality was reflected in the curriculum itself. Within a framework of Jewish scholarship there was no set curriculum. Each student was privileged to study whatever he chose, according to his own capacities and background, at his own pace, setting his own limits; and this is a procedure he followed all his life. There were no degrees, no grades, no hierarchy of classes to spur him on, to tell him how he was doing, to place him in a comparative scale of achievement. There was no graduation, no end; the certificate he could ask for if he wanted to teach was only functional—it did not state that he had completed his studies. Study was never completed; it merely ceased at death.

Above all, there was no textbook. From *kheder* to grave, the Jews worked with primary sources, treating them as data to examine, question, analyze, interpret, infer from; not as unquestioned authority. And the expert, in our current conception of the term, simply could not exist. A man could question even the word of God and could examine it for hidden meanings; each man interpreted it for himself, uniquely. The only "how-to" which the Jews consented to learn consisted of the minutely detailed rules of conduct in the Talmud; and even these, each felt entitled to interpret for himself, according to each particular situation.

So the development of the potential to learn became for these people an exciting adventure, a pitting of wits and learning, a searching for buried meanings, a drawing of firmly founded conclusions from data, eliciting the respect of family and community, filling the role of the Jewish male, fulfilling man's obligation to God. It is no wonder that individuals devoted themselves to this development from *kheder* to grave, at the expense of comfort, good food, ease, material possessions.

To my mind, the secret lies in the supporting values of the home and the community, as well as in the encouragement of a questioning mind, of a mind that demands the right to come to its own conclusions. It does not lie in the specifics of the social organization or of the cultural pattern; and certainly not in the pedagogical principles of the beginning *kheder*. When the *kheder* disappears, when the *shtetl* is left behind, when shoes are on the feet and a warm meal comes at noon, we still get the overwhelming effort and the inquiring mind. I believe that it is no accident that so many of the outstanding men in the world of letters in recent years have been Jews—men like Freud and Thomas Mann and Franz Boas, the father of anthropology in this country. Statistically, the number does not make sense. The specifics of the *shtetl* may have disappeared, but the all-embracing, permeating value, and the emphasis on the questioning spirit remain, producing these great figures. Einstein, for instance, did not live in a *shtetl* and never went to a *kheder*. He was brought up in a tradition which he did not recognize as Jewish until he was a grown man. Nevertheless, his family afforded a weekly meal to a student, a Russian Jew, whose only claim was that he was a Jewish student. Education was highly valued in this home, though it was not rooted in religious responsibility.

I should like to add that in this country the large number of Jews in the academic and other professions is out of all proportion with the population of some four and a half million Jews that was estimated for 1948. I realize that here I am treading on questionable ground. I am not supposed to distinguish Jews from the rest of the American population. To do so raises the specter of discrimination. And indeed, in the attempt to avoid discrimination, we usually ask no questions as to cultural grouping, and so we have no statistics on Jews in the national census and other such sources. The figure I gave you, and the figures I will give you below have been arrived at deviously and with great difficulty. To find out the number of Jews in their cities, study groups had to resort to such means as getting the number of children absent from school on Yom Kippur, comparing it with the usual number of daily absences, and inferring the number of the Jewish population from the number of additional absences on Yom Kippur.

We are so afraid that discrimination will lead to derogation, that we make no distinctions in our records; yet the Jews distinguish themselves on their own; they simply stand out of the national averages. In New York, the highly competitive Bronx High School of Science is largely Jewish. In the country at large, the percentage of Jews who have attended college or received post-graduate degrees appears to be two to three times as great as that of the total white population; and locally the difference is sometimes even greater. In 1948, for instance, a study in New Orleans showed that "almost no Jews failed to get further than elementary school but one-fifth of all whites from sixteen to twenty-five had less than eight years of schooling." Eighty percent of the Jews had attended college a minimum of one year as against 25 percent of the total white population.

I have given here a biased view of learning in other cultures. As I said earlier, I deliberately selected the Oglala and the Eastern European Jews for presentation because they exhibit so strongly values making for the development of this capacity to learn. I do not present them as a random sample; these values are not present everywhere. What I have tried to bring out is that the values were so influential because they were consistently expressed and because they permeated all life; and, secondly, that in their strength they overcame possible drawbacks in the educational system. If this is so, then it follows that the interference with development comes through the absence or weakness of such values, or through inconsistency among the various aspects of the culture.

I have sometimes horrified my listeners or readers in describing the education of the Sioux and particularly the literate education in the *shtetl*. Besides pity for them, the question always arose as to what kind of mental health did these children grow up to have. They had no period of childhood, or irresponsibility, of purposeless play, none of what is essential to the making of a healthy human being.

The first and, to some extent, the slightest answer I would give to these, is that there was play, particularly among the Sioux. When little Hakadah went out to "look carefully at everything" he saw in the morning, he met his friends. He liked to be alone, but he also liked to be with his friends, swim or run races or climb rocks. Of course, this was learning skills and strengthening the muscles so that through competition they could go even beyond their ordinary strength; "but" they were fun. I put the "but" in quotation marks because for me it is not a but. Ohiyesa (which is the name Hakadah later earned for himself) describes later the life in the tepee in the evening where there were jokes, funny stories, teasing, people shaking with laughter.

A young, white trader from a neighboring tribe tells of how his Indian wife shakes him awake one morning at dawn saying "Get up, get up, it is a good day to be alive."

For me, it is this that constitutes mental health. Perhaps, also, the play and the jokes and the laughter; but finding the day "a good day to be alive" is for me a stronger test of mental health than the question of whether Hakadah was working or playing. We usually distinguish work from play by calling "play" something which is nonpurposive. To me, when play is called nonpurposive, this often means that it is not fulfilling a purpose which the adult recognizes. In such a case it is nonsense to ask whether, and when, Hakadah is playing or working. I don't know what to call his experience of teaching himself, when he was alert and sensitive to everything around him, infinitely involved—what shall I call this?

As to the *shtetl* scholars in the United States, I believe you all know as much as I do. In Sholem Aleichem's autobiographic writings the boys who go to school do not seem entirely grim; they joke, they seem to find some time to play.

I have been stressing childhood play as well as laughter and joking simply because they are considered an important part of mental health. However, I believe there are other aspects of mental health that may be even more vital. When a bearded scholar in the *shtetl* seriously discussed a subject with a young boy, contradicting him, bringing up scholarly arguments against him, he honors the selfhood of the boy. In the discussion there is no "kindness" or condescension shown. For me, the fact that a little boy is recognized as a person with his own right to think and to come up with new interpretations and new suggestions which will be listened to with intent interest—this, to me, is a very important aspect of mental health.

When the boys were ready to read and understand Hebrew, they chose a commentary to which to give a new interpretation, their own, one never given before. They chose their own, and decided for themselves when that particular section of their education was over. They showed that they believed in themselves, that they valued their own thinking and own judgment. As I have said, for me this is an important, perhaps the most important, aspect of mental health: valuing of one's own, original thinking, sensing, judging, and the ability to be completely involved in it.

Out of the experience of boys in the *shtetl* and among the Sioux I would like to keep for my children the self-love and infinity of involvement, but also give them the opportunity of playing out of doors. Perhaps the child will be furiously involved in digging, or building, or learning a new skipping step—whether we want to call this "learning" or "play," he is certainly living and growing.

BIBLIOGRAPHY

Oglala Sioux

BROWN, JOSEPH EPES. *The Sacred Pipe, Black Elk's Account of the Seven Rites of the Oglala Sioux.* Recorded and edited by Joseph Epes Brown. Norman: University of Oklahoma Press, 1953.

EASTMAN, CHARLES A. (Ohiyesa). *An Indian Boyhood.* Boston: Little, Brown & Company, 1902.

———. *The Soul of an Indian.* Boston: Houghton Mifflin Company, 1911.

STANDING BEAR, LUTHER. *My People the Sioux.* Boston: Houghton Mifflin Company, 1928.

———. *Land of the Spotted Eagle.* Boston: Houghton Mifflin Company, 1932.

Eastern European Jews

ALEICHEM, SHOLOM. *The Great Fair. Scenes from My Childhood.* Translated by Tamara Kahana. The Noonday Press, New York, 1955.

BARUCH, BERNARD M. *Baruch: My Own Story.* New York: Henry Holt & Company, 1957.

COHEN, MORRIS RAPHAEL. *A Dreamer's Journey.* The Beacon Press. Boston, Mass., 1949.

GORDON, ALBERT I. *Jews in Transition.* Minneapolis: University of Minnesota Press, 1949.

SKLARE, MARSHALL, ed. *The Jews. Social Patterns of an American Group.* Glencoe, Ill.: The Free Press, 1958.

ZBOROWSKI, MARK. "The Place of Book Learning in Traditional Jewish Culture" in *Childhood in Contemporary Cultures.* Edited by Margaret Mead and M. Wolfenstein. Chicago: University of Chicago Press, 1955.

ZBOROWSKI, MARK and HERZOG, ELIZABETH. *Life Is with People*. New York: International University Press, Inc., 1952.

Chinese

SZE, MAI-MAI. *The Tao of Painting: A Study of the Ritual Disposition of Chinese Painting*. With a translation of the *Mustard Seed Garden Manual of Painting*. New York: Pantheon Books, 1956.
SPINDLER, GEORGE DEARBORN. *The Transmission of American Culture*. Cambridge, Mass.: Harvard University Press, 1959.

FREEDOM AND SOCIAL CONSTRAINT

I shall speak first of social constraint and then freedom. My thesis is:

1. That social constraint may exist only in the observer's eye; in such a case it would be irrelevant to the freedom of the individuals in the society observed.

2. That phenomenologically it may be not constraint but structure; that is, the observed individual may be experiencing it as enabling, for instance; as affording a map to make procedure possible, and thus giving clarification. In such a case, therefore, it would be experienced as something relevant to the very conditions of freedom.

3. That the absence of constraint in itself does not mean that the individual is, therefore, free to choose to act or be.

In the second part of this chapter I shall describe what I mean by the conditions of freedom and by freedom itself; and this shall be followed by a presentation of material from other cultures, to show how the individual is evoked to freedom in other societies.

In writing the preceding sentence, I observed a number of taboos and followed a number of regulations. I refrained from using obscenity or any particularly strong language. I refrained from using colloquial English. In fact I also resisted the temptation of

"Freedom and Social Constraint," by Dorothy Lee. From David Bidney, ed., *The Concept of Freedom in Anthropology* (The Hague: Mouton & Co., Publishers, 1963), pp. 61-73. Reprinted by permission of the publisher. Originally a paper delivered at the Wenner-Gren Foundations Symposium, Burg Wartenstein, Austria, August 3-11, 1961.

substituting a Greek word for an English word, even though my knowledge of Greek is as good as that of English. I put in a comma where the rule of my culture posits a comma; I added an *s* to "culture" by way of following the rule that more than one culture should be referred to by means of an added *s*. I followed a large number of regulations pertaining to vocabulary, grammar, academic communication, etc. However, until I started writing the first section I was not even aware I had been following all these regulations and observing all these taboos.

I am starting with this example because I actually took on this structure myself as a series of regulations and taboos; I learned English out of a grammar book, out of a dictionary, and out of the drilling of my teacher. Even so, by now the structure has been internalized and is now a guiding principle within me; a principle of which I am not conscious, without which, as a matter of fact, I could not have been free to write this book. For most of the people who do speak in English, particularly when they speak the English idiom used in their own family, the "constraint" was never present as a series of regulations; they learned the regulations in school long after they had been communicating freely in English.

I believe this is true of all aspects of culture. For instance, now that we have become sophisticated about our own culture in the United States, we speak of time-binding. I myself speak about slavery to time schedule. We are constrained by the date, the hour, the deadline. Yet, when I get up in the morning, how do I know what to do? How can I act freely without being ordered by someone else to do what has to be done? Actually I do act autonomously, just because I have a schedule. If I know the date and the time of day, and if I know my schedule, I know how to proceed. If it is Tuesday, November 23, I dress in time to go to teach my class at 9 o'clock. If it is Thursday, November 25, I go to my kitchen to stuff the turkey for Thanksgiving dinner. If, when I wake up, my clock says 5, I turn around and sleep some more. If it says 8, I get up. No one has to order me to get up, or to go back to sleep.

My time schedule, the clarity of the structure within which I find myself—that is, the "social constraint"—not only frees me from the interference of others, but actually makes it possible for me to act; that is, it furnishes me with the conditions of freedom. If I wake up after a period of amnesia and do not know whether it is October or May, twilight or dawn, Wednesday or Sunday, I am truly constrained. I am immobilized. I do not know even what to eat if I am hungry. Should I have toast and orange juice, eggs and bacon, or should I have roast beef and potatoes and ice cream for dessert?

Perhaps I am not even entirely sure that I am hungry; that is, I am not sure that my hunger is valid and should be recognized. Should I recognize these feelings as hunger at 3:30 in the afternoon? Or should I suspect this of being the beginning of an upset stomach? Or should I simply dull the pangs with a snack?

As a detached observer, studying my own culture, I can still call this time-binding; I can still call this constraint. But when I am involved in this life, when I live in dialogue with this structure, I experience it as a condition of freedom. It makes it possible for me to proceed in what would otherwise be a confusing jungle; it makes it possible for me to function. My students from non-Western societies, and even from some other Western societies, find me unbelievably constrained when they first arrive in this country. They put themselves in my place and find me intolerably coerced; but of course, they have brought their own culture with them when they have put "themselves" in "my" place. They look from the outside and find constraint; I from the inside find this to be a way of life, a clear trail.

Social "constraint" for me, then, is structure, necessary for life itself. My image of it is that of the system of girders of a skyscraper that is going up, or of the skeleton of a vertebrate, affording form and caliber and direction; giving meaning and limit to growth. And here I should add that I use the term *limit* only because I can find no other. I do not mean to imply by this an external obstruction, a cutting off of growth, or even "limitation." I mean by it something like a meaningful cessation of growth in a certain direction, helping to give definition to that which would otherwise have been inchoate and ambiguous.

I have just used the word *definition*. A few lines above I used the term *limit*. Both of these words can be viewed as constraint; and yet I have used them to refer to the opposite of constraint. . . .

Does the removal of constraint mean freedom? In the last century, when the issue of slavery was in the forefront in the United States, freedom certainly meant removal of constraint; it meant deliverance from slavery. In many parts of the world freedom has meant and still means deliverance from oppressive monarchy, or from colonial rule. In such cases freedom does refer to the removal of political constraint and social constraint. And it is possible that such constraint carried to an extreme may cut off all avenues of the exertion of the self, and thus atrophy existence itself.

However, I question that the removal of constraint would, therefore, mean freedom. Simply withholding from me the constraint against moving or singing does not mean that I shall, therefore, feel free to move or sing. Furnishing me with a violin, and removing the rule against playing the violin, does not mean that I am, therefore, free to play or even free to want to play the violin. Removal of constraint and so-called freedom of opportunity are irrelevant if there is no urge to do, act, choose, perhaps even if the urge, while present, is not encouraged in some way.

In my view, freedom is an aspect of being, or a quality of being itself. Freedom lies where *be* becomes *to be;* where the vague, the timeless, the not-phenomenal, the unasserted, is transformed into an assertion, at the point when the individual *chooses* to be, to walk, to think, to suffer, to see. It is at this point that he lives freely, that he is in an active state of freedom. And unless constraint is complete, and unless it eventually manages to kill the thrust to be, it is irrelevant to freedom. If within himself the individual is not free, the absence of constraint will not mean freedom.

Conversely, we have occasions of apparently absolute constraint in which the individual has been known to assert his freedom. Such, I believe, was the situation on certain occasions in Nazi concentration camps when Jews who were completely constrained, oppressed, and driven, who had had all their belongings, their clothing, even the very hair of their bodies, that is all the trappings of their identity removed from them; a people whose names had been taken from them and replaced by numbers; people who had been starved and tortured and coerced into all sorts of unnameable indignities; such was the situation when these people could still choose to act as free men, raising their voices to sing on their march to enforced extermination.

It has taken me years of intensive work with other cultures to arrive at the position where I see freedom as not necessarily related to constraint. For instance, when I first read *The Tale of Genji*, I was appalled at the extent to which life was dictated to the women of the nobility and to Genji himself. A woman knew that she must write a morning-after letter to Genji. The form of the letter was prescribed, the content was traditional; the kind of paper, the ink, the calligraphy were all given. When it came to Genji, I found out that at any ceremonial occasion his costume, its form, its color, the very underwear he put on were all established for him. When I put myself into this culture I felt terribly constrained and unfree. But I soon realized what was wrong. I had put *myself* in this situation.

So I reread *The Tale of Genji*, trying to feel it as it must have been experienced by Lady Murasaki's characters. I saw that when Genji opened the morning-after letter he read it and valued it according to the freedom, the self-assertion, the originality, the individuality of the writer. I saw that Lady Murasaki herself was presenting Genji as someone free, as someone prized by all around because of his thrusting freedom. There were the men who, unlike Genji, simply moved along the predetermined grooves; and these men were not valued. There were the women who wrote their morning-after letter in placid conformity to the rule and these Genji found dull. But there were also the free spirits who could use the regulations in such a way that they could reach freedom, that they could choose to act, to assert their being. When freedom was there, "constraint"—that is, what I felt as constraint—could neither stop it nor kill it. The rules were not circumvented, they were used as channels of creative expression.

Again I was shocked when I first read Bowie's *On the Laws of Japanese Painting.* I found out that the pictures I had admired so much were actually composed of pre-established shapes, relations, groups of lines; I found out that even the shape of the space between two leaves of plantain was prescribed. Was there no originality in Japanese painting? I found out that the Japanese artist was not "free" to paint a chrysanthemum in the spring; and what if he felt like doing this? Was not this rule an intolerable constraint? And then I saw, as I believe Bowie suggests, that what the Japanese artist was being offered was a set of rules only, as I am offered the rules of English grammar. If he chose to paint, if he was free to paint, he could use these rules in the way that I use grammar when I am writing this paper. He could use it in such a way that he could express his own style, his idiosyncracy. Damon Runyon and T. S. Eliot use the same rules of grammar and vocabulary; but no one can mistake the style of one for that of the other. And it is only because e. e. cummings has made the rules of grammar completely his own, that he can transcend them so that he can say "the gay illimitably earth."

I have been speaking so far about social constraint. I have maintained that it does not touch man's freedom; it neither prevents the thrust of freedom nor does it provoke it. However, what I say about social constraint does not apply to culture, in my view. I believe that the cultural framework itself, the symbolic world of the society into which the individual is born and into which he is introduced by his society does have a high relevance to human freedom.

I believe that man is born with the capacity to be free. As I did earlier, I find the words furnished to me by the English language inadequate here, and later I hope to show in what respect the opening sentence of this paragraph is misleading. For the present, however, I shall let this sentence stand.

I shall now return to my reference to the freedom of playing the violin and shall discuss it at some length. Let us say that I am born with the capacity to be free to play the violin. Unless my culture furnishes me with the opportunity—that is, unless there are violins around or I am told that they exist, I obviously cannot actualize this capacity. If my society, if the people I respect and love value violin music and the making of violin music, I shall probably want to learn how to play the instrument. This is not enough. I must also have instruction in the different positions of fingering and in bowing; I must have the support and the encouragement to commit myself to the long and intense discipline involved. I shall even have to expand the span of what David Bidney has called my biological freedom: I shall have to increase the sheer physical strength of my muscles, the stretch of my fingers; my hearing will have to be trained in discrimination and in sensitive discernment.

My society furnishes me with all these conditions which are necessary to actualize my freedom. Let us say it even respects my right to play the violin. Does this mean that I, therefore, play the violin? Not necessarily. Something must be there, before "I know how to play," "I can play," becomes "I play," "I choose to play." I need to be evoked to play. Perhaps if I have an audience who really wants to hear me play, or perhaps if I have a group of friends who depend on me to form a chamber group with them; or if I passionately want to translate the notes on the pages into music heard and felt, then I choose to play.

According to my view of freedom, the conditions of freedom are not enough. Unless I *choose* to play, I am not free. I must find in my cultural framework in addition to the conditions, that conception of myself in society, or of myself in dialogue with the universe, which will evoke the thrust so that "I can play" will be transformed to "I up and play."

The cultural systems I have studied all included some conditions of freedom; in each case these were concentrated in that area which is of prime value in the particular society which lives by this culture; at any rate, this was true at the time they were described. Each cultural system has amazed me with the tremendous amount and detail and complexity and precision of knowledge which it offered the individual member of the society, the diversity and intensity of training and self-discipline it demanded. Judging by the autobiographies of these societies, this body of knowledge, this course of increasing hardihood, was often sought as a privilege.

All this complexity and precision was learned, all the self-discipline was undertaken without great outside pressure, without a system of external rewards and punishments, without the society's attempt to furnish motivation.

Each society trained in its own way, presenting its staggering curriculum, developing the capacities necessary for free functioning, chosen functioning, in its own valued area. Consider for instance the minuteness and sheer number of details which the Nyakyusa have to master for carrying out the rituals of kinship. These may revolve around the continuity with the lineage, with maintaining the continuity, or creating a new one. They may be concerned with protecting one's mother from the potency of one's husband's lineage, or with preventing the contamination which threatens if two lineages were to meet in the body of a woman or a new-born infant. They center upon the prime value of the society; and they seem to be learned as a matter of course, the way one learns to carry a water pot, or herd, or hoe.

I could multiply such instances from different parts of the world. I shall limit myself to the Indians of the Western United States, about whom I shall speak in greater detail below. Among the Dakota, the emphasis was on relatedness with all aspects of the universe, culminating in the ultimate leap to the Great Design, a leap requiring unbelievable endurance of pain, hunger, thirst, fear of danger; so here the systematic training from birth on was such that the individual could be free to function in this area. Earlier we saw how Standing Bear, an Oglala Dakota, as a boy of three or so was taught to strengthen and sharpen his senses, to perceive and observe and discriminate, so that he could become acquainted with his relatives: the meadow lark, the ant, the thunder, the rock. Charles Eastman (Ohiyesa), a Santee Dakota, shows how and with what meticulous care and concern he was taught to draw conclusions and inductions from his observations, and to arrive at moral choice and ethical judgment on the basis of a known situation. He shows how he was taught the nature of sacrifice, and beyond this, *to* sacrifice, to choose to sacrifice, to deepen his relatedness to the universe.

These men, as well as other Dakota who were born in the latter part of the last century, describe the hardships to which they readily exposed themselves, and which in fact they courted as little boys and later as young men by way of growing in hardihood. They broke the ice on the surface of the pool or stream in early morning to plunge in for a stinging bath; they walked many hours a day in snow that came halfway up their hips. When there was a rainstorm in the winter, young men would joyously strip and rush out into the cold downpour. Indians from other tribes tell similar stories. Navaho men have given us accounts of how they developed their capacity for hardihood. They speak of how boys of eight, who, in the beginning were awakened by others to run before daylight, soon undertook to find their own ways of intensifying their exertion. One man tells of how he used to put sand in his moccasins; or how, in the summer he elected to run in the midday sun. In the winter, boys would roll naked in the snow, run with ice in their mouths, plunge in ice-crusted streams. At one time, three boys decided not to sleep for forty-eight hours. Boys might decide to fast; or they might get together, put plant powder on the backs of their hands and burn it; increasing gradually the span of their endurance.

These exercises in discipline are equivalent to the long and arduous hours which my daughter spent learning to play the violin, concentrating at the age of eight on one note, the same unvaried note, for forty minutes, trying to get her bowing to the point where she was satisfied with it. This discipline, however, whether offered as a system of procedure, or whether self-imposed training, is still only a condition necessary to freedom; it is not freedom itself.

Yet there is something of what I have called freedom even in the accounts I have referred to here. In official American culture, the assumption is that no one on his own initiative will undertake the necessary discipline, no one will do hard work, expose himself to dullness and monotony, to discomfort or pain, to exertion without established limit, freely, at his own choice. As a child, he has to be coerced with threat or with punishment itself, or prodded with the promise of reward, of approval, or of the satisfaction of outdoing a rival. Motivation is conceived of as a motor to be installed, since the urge presumably does not exist in the individual. No one is expected to choose to create his own conditions of freedom.

In the American Indian cultures of which I have spoken, on the other hand, the individual freely, autonomously, chooses to enable himself to live freely. No one nags him to practice, no one offers him an *A* for learning the list of the presidents of the United States. According to the Dakota autobiographies, the world was presented to the individual from birth on in such a way that becoming skilled and disciplined, the learning to function in the Dakota world, becoming worthy of relatedness to the wind or the ant or the Great Spirit, was as much of an act of choice as functioning itself.

What accounted for this choosing to be and become, I think, was the cultural conception of man as an open system in transaction with the universe—to use an inclusive and deliberately vague term—as also an open system. I believe that this conception of man was held in different specific forms throughout the entire world of non-Western civilization. I should add that I am only suggesting that this is so. I have made intensive studies of only a few American Indian cultures and even fewer Oceanic cultures; and I have not been able to get any consistent picture of the symbolic worlds of Africa. The study necessary to penetrate into another symbolic world requires years of intensive and incisive work, and besides there are all too few societies which have been observed and recorded with the sensitivity that makes it possible to investigate questions of existence. However, what I do know of those cultures which have not been reported on fully enough for intensive study, or which I have not been able to study fully, and what I do know of non-Western civilizations in general makes me suspect that only in Western culture man was assumed to be in a closed system; and that this has been increasingly the case in the Newtonian era. I have wondered—but have not been able to investigate this— whether the fatalism of the Mohammedan world, for instance, is not an invention of students who can perceive and conceive only in terms of closed systems.

What I find, for instance, among the Eskimo and among the American Indian societies which I have studied intensively, is a view of a universe as something unfinished, imperfect; I find a conception of a world which in fact does not exist, is not a world, without man's perceiving, conceptualizing, experiencing. In such a world there are no sensations—closed systems impinging upon closed systems—but rather creative acts of perception. There are no symbols, there are acts of symbolization. Here man does not adjust *to*, does not adapt himself to his environment, because the environment does not "environ." And in fact, alone, in monologue, man *is* not; and the "environment" does not exist without his experience of it, his concern for it. There is interpenetration, but more than that, what penetrates is in the making and makes in the process of being made. I believe that this constant call to create and create oneself is what evokes man to freedom—to choose to act; to change *be* to *I am* or *it is*.

The image of the world as imperfect, and of that which is given to man's experience as imperfect, to be progressively perfected by man while creating himself, does exist also in the Western world. It is not part of official American culture; that is, it is only sporadically present in the public school system or in the business world, for instance. However, where it does exist, I believe it is viewed as inviting man to freedom, to choosing to act. It is the basis underlying true seminar teaching; and "teaching" in this context is a glaringly wrong term. Our artists, as I have said, are articulating this view when they ask for the reader or the viewer or the hearer to be a collaborator, an accomplice, in creating the novel or the picture or the musical composition.

In a recent paper on "The Imperfect Tense in the Poema Del Cid," Stephen Gilman shows how the "juglar" uses the imperfect by way of involving his audience: "What the imperfect seems to do is display sentiment for our *participation*" (italics my own) and engages us in the contemplation of "movement going on—movement which in its incompletion seems to absorb, to carry along with it the heroic mover." To translate into the terms I used above, the audience is conceived as an open system in transaction with the "heroic mover" as an open system; and this imperfection is an invitation to the audience to engage in that which is being presented, to choose to respond.

The preterit, on the other hand, is used by the juglar, according to Stephen Gilman, for something finished and presented for our admiration—not for our collaboration; it is a closed system presented to closed systems.

In the Indian and Eskimo societies on this continent, to which I referred above, this view of man and situation as imperfect in themselves, is more pervasive, clearer, basic. In a recent study of the Eskimo, for instance, Paul Riesman shows that for these people, man is a collaborator with the rest of the universe in creating the Eskimo world of existence. According to Paul Riesman, for the Eskimo the universe is thought, but man only has the capacity to think. Yet man cannot think unless thought enters him, and thought cannot exist unless man thinks it. If I say, then, that thought exists outside man, every one of the words I use is wrong, because I use them in the context of my culture where man is complete in himself, the universe is complete in itself, and thought either exists or does not exist. For the Eskimo thought outside man does not have existence, it hovers on the brink of existence; in fact it is not thought, it does not exist, it is not outside, since the universe itself contains man, and man is not man completely without the so-called outside.

We find a similar conception of the universe among Indians, such as the Navaho and the Hopi. For instance, it is apparent through the Navaho linguistic structure, that when a man "rolled" a ball, this was an effective but not a transitive act. The ball contained the rollingness and man joined his operation to this before the ball could roll.

And the Hopi Way was a systematic expression of such a view. Raining-ness had to be transformed into raining by man through his ceremonial, for instance; that is, it was not man's function to force the clouds to discharge their rain, but rather to furnish the necessary factor in completing the whole, in actualizing the design.

For myself, I have found this assumption expressed in the linguistic structure of the Wintu language; and I give here a brief account of how this is expressed.

Let us take the word *debu*. By itself this word means *cross*; that is, cross a stream, a ridge, or even from underground to above ground. I say it means *cross*; yet we feel uncomfortable with "cross" alone. We are tempted to supply something to complete it: make it into *I* cross, or at least *to* cross. But, in fact, the "cross" is at the other end from these forms, it is absolutely different from them. When it is self-complete it functions as the equivalent of our imperative; but, for reasons into which I cannot go at length here, I think that it is not even an admonition. It certainly does not express the imposing of the will of one person upon another person.

Now the person who hears *debu*, addressed to him or who otherwise relates himself to *debu*, transforms this into *diba* through his act of will. He changes *cross* into *to cross*. He says *diba-da*, I have just crossed, or I do cross; or he says, *diba-wida*, I intend to or I will (to) cross; or *diba-ise-da*, I crossed in the recent past, etc. He has taken the potential, and through his own act of choice, through his assertive experience, he has brought this into history; he has actualized this. I must hasten to say, however, that what I have called "potential" was incompletely so; it was potential only insofar as man was ready to respond to it in the process of his own becoming.

Except as the Wintu equivalent of our own imperative, the word *debu* is never used alone. Most frequently it is used with the suffix *-le(·s)*. I found this most confusing when I first started analysing my texts. My Wintu informants translated it variously as *must, shall, can, may* and *before* (in a sequence of acts). It was also translated as *so as to, or to*, but only on occasions where man did not act as agent; for instance in *to die*, but not in *to commit suicide*.

Presently I found this frightening. It seemed to me that man was rigidly constrained by necessity, a passive creature to whom events happened. How else could I explain the sequence I logically formed? That: what may be, can be, must be and shall come to be.

Where was man in all this? Where was agency, choice, will? In 1934 I wrote that this referred to a world of events which existed and took place irrespective of man.

It took me many years to realize that this, in fact, was just the opposite of what was implied; that none of this had existence or could come into existence, without man, irrespective of man. Of course, I had to see it as I did, because I saw it against the logic of my own culture. Man could not be both agent and passive recipient of a happening. He could not, in the same act be initiating, giving rise to an occurrence and at the same time carrying out the pre-ordained. I saw the factors in these dualisms as finished, complete and mutually exclusive. So, I saw the term *debu* as referring to an existing state which *must* happen to passive man; that is, I saw it as "it *is*" instead of "*be*"; irrespective of man instead of needing man's agency before it could be translated into "it is." I saw it as completed, closed, happening to a complete person; when it was instead imperfect, a suggested design, when, in fact, it *was not*. Even to call it "possible" would be to misrepresent it; because it was possible only insofar as man was willing to act. The distinctions which I had carefully made in translating the -*le·s* simply were not there; I had invented them and introduced them. What had appalled and frightened me had been a creature of my own phantasy. These distinctions could exist only in my own symbolic world.

Now, I see the Wintu image of man-in-universe as an evocation to freedom. I can see this even when I translate the -*le·s* into my own terms with all my precise distinctions. For if a man chooses to act, then of course what *can* be *must* be, since only this chosen act of man was lacking for its perfection; and, naturally, then it *shall* be, coming into being through man's act. Providing the conditions of freedom are there—providing the hunter has disciplined himself in huntsmanship, carries out the appropriate ceremonial and is permitted to hunt, etc.—this symbolic world of imperfect-man-in-transaction-with-imperfect-universe, each inviting the other to collaborate in its completion, engenders freedom itself.

I said earlier that I believe that man is born with the capacity to be free. I should like to say now that this should be seen in the context of the imperfect; that even the capacity itself *is* not; it only *be*, unless man is evoked to freedom.

TO BE OR NOT TO BE

Notes on the Meaning of Maternity

When I make a decision *to be*, to be a mother, I make, at the same time, in the same act, the decision that a child is to be. Maternity is a relationship. So also, when I decide that a new life is to come into being, I make a decision for myself—to be Mother and not just a mother. I may think of myself as a mother already; I "have" other children. So actually my decision is not "to be a mother" but to be mother-to-this-child. I shall talk here about these two ends of the continuum, or if you will, these two effects of my decision *to be*.

My culture does nothing to help me in viewing my decision in this way; in fact, it interferes. For instance, my language encourages me to see myself as *having*, possessing, a baby. Now, nothing of what I have said above is expressed in the phrase "I have a son." On the other hand, the Wintu Indians, whose language I recorded, can never say "I have a son." In fact, they never say "*a* son" or "*a* mother." Instead, they say "a-her-son" and "a-his-mother," always bringing to notice both ends of the relatedness. For, how can a woman be *a* mother unless she is *somebody's* mother? I shall speak then of the continuum, with its two ends, that comes into being at the moment when a woman conceives a child.

First of all, when I become a mother, when *I* bring into

"To Be or Not to Be: Notes on the Meaning of Maternity," by Dorothy Lee. From Seymour M. Farber and Roger H. L. Wilson, eds., *The Challenge to Women* (New York: Basic Books, Inc., Publishers, 1966), pp. 51–62. Copyright © 1966 by Basic Books, Inc., Publishers. Reprinted by permission of the publisher.

being—of course in cooperation—this new relationship, it is *I* who becomes a mother. It is impossible to be nothing but a mother or a wife. If it is impossible to be a mother unless I am somebody's mother, it is also impossible for me to achieve motherhood unless I am somebody to begin with. First of all, *I* have to be. I say this knowing also that at this time, in this year, there are many women who simply *are not*, who are nothing, or who do not know that they exist; women who out of their emptiness think that they will find some anchor in life, can put down some root into life through having a child. I think there is possibly an increasing number of these women in a society that offers an increasingly empty life to its members. Men try to fill the emptiness with their own clutter; women often try to fill it with what turns out to be human clutter. I think there is probably an increasing number of women who use childbearing as a way to fill the frightening emptiness.

I would like to say to these women: "Do not have a child unless, first of all, you come to be yourself, unless first of all *you are.* You are doing something terrible to your child if you use him as a means to an end, and also to yourself, because now your life will be filled with worry, instead of commitment, experience, growth, meaning." Of course, I cannot say this, because these women would probably not know what I am talking about. To women in general, I would like to say that if they decide to become mothers only because of the lack in their lives, only because of the frightening emptiness, I do not think that they will become mother in more than a biological sense; because motherhood, if it is more than a biological fact, if it is a relationship between person and person, has to have two ends to the relationship. For this, I have to exist as a person.

If this is taken into account—that is, that motherhood is a new dimension of an already existing person—then when a woman makes a decision as to whether to become a mother or not, whether to go on with her profession while she is a wife and mother, whether to come back to take a graduate course or college courses or other education at the time when she has little children, she makes it on the basis of whether this will strengthen and enhance her and develop her as a person, whether this will enrich her existence. And this is not selfish. It is vital, in fact indispensable, for the relationship. The one thing that a woman or any person has to give to the world and to the people with whom she is intimate is her individual person—her self in growth, in adventure, in search, in reaching out to her environment. She owes it to her family, to society, to develop this. And this is the basis on which she decides to confine herself to her family and her home, or to go out for further study or a job.

Motherhood is not a thing in itself, it is *I* who am a mother and I have to *be myself* first.

Before I take up the other end of the continuum, there is one more point I would like to make. When I choose to be a mother, I choose for the world; my decision changes the character and composition of the world. To illustrate this blatantly I will ask you to think of the decision of the mother of Einstein, or Marx, or Hitler, or Schweitzer, or the mother of the little boy next door. To the woman who believes in God, I would say she chooses for God, because God cannot create a child without her help, nor can God create a meaningful life for the child without her help. When she decides to be a mother in the full sense, she collaborates with God and enables Him to actualize His will. To recognize this means to be impressed by the significance and tremendous seriousness of the decision to have a child.

Secondly, as I have said above, when a woman is a mother she is somebody's mother, she is the mother of an individual, or rather of someone who has the inalienable right to be an individual. She is not simply a mother and she is not, of course, a mother of "children," but she is a mother of *this* child, of a second child, and a third child—she does not become a mother once and for all.

I like the way a Wintu in reference to his mother will say, "she-whom-I-made-into-mother," even though he is the fourth child. I like it because it gives recognition to the fact that this is not a repetition of the same event. A new mother has been born, mother-to-*this*-child, and a new relationship of motherness has come into being. When this is recognized, the mother is helped to sense the particularity of her child, and the peculiar flavor, the peculiar quality of the relationship that she can have with each child. It is good to "have children," it is good to see one's self as the mother of children, but it is also necessary, I think, to recognize and to develop the relationship that greets personally the individuality of each child.

When a woman who is a person decides to be a mother, she decides to continue being a person—a person who is also a mother. This does not mean that she is not fully a mother. She is fully mother in a qualitative sense, not in a quantitative sense. For instance, she has to be all there when she is with her children, in the same way that if she drives on a Los Angeles freeway she has to be all there or die. But it does not mean she is always driving on a Los Angeles freeway—God forbid. It means that there is a certain quality of utter alertness, of full attention, of undistractable concentration. It means that all her capacities are available to her, ready to be drawn upon; that her senses are striving to receive the messages that her child is sending out to her. It means that she is all there when she is with her child, sharing an unadulterated experience with him. It does not mean that she has to be a practicing mother all her time.

Now this, for me, has something to do with the question: "How many children will I have? Will I have two? Six?" If my relation to my child is such as I have described above, I cannot think of my children as something to count. In a sense, they are unique and unrepeatable events, not objects.

There is much said nowadays about the prevalence of number. For myself, I do not object to being a number for the Federal Government, or my insurance company, or my bank; it makes matters simpler and more efficient yet leaves my personal integrity intact. What is terrible to me is when I am a number in my human relations; when I think of my children as numbers or am myself treated as one, anyone, out of twenty or a hundred. There are societies where, when mothers are asked by the ethnographer how many children they have, they say they do not know; and eventually, the social scientist satisfies his Western need to know the number by collecting all the names of all the children and counting them for himself. In other societies, where numbers are used, they are ordinal: this is my second son, that is the third daughter. This way, they are not referred to as interchangeable.

We speak a lot about uniqueness these days, and I am afraid I too will have to use this stale word. But our culture does not encourage or help us to give recognition to uniqueness. For instance, mothers are told that they should recognize the "difference" in each of their children. But to try to know a person in terms of what he is not is a lazy attempt to know, and all I achieve is the recognition that in fact my child is not like someone else. But I still do not know my child. I can tell you in what ways this apple differs from an elephant, or a pear or a cloud or a stone, or even another apple. But I do not know the apple unless I enter into a pure, clear, interpenetrating relationship with it. Not with any apple—with *this* apple. And the joy I get out of contemplating its curve and color, out of smelling its fragrance, or out of its crispness between my teeth, and its juiciness and flavor, has nothing to do with its difference. In relating to it I know it as *this*. But if I am preoccupied or uninterested I see nothing but *an* apple, any apple; in fact, I don't see it. Now you can take it away and replace it by another, and I probably won't notice; if I do "notice the difference," it is only this I notice. I do not know what was there before nor what is there now; only that there is a difference.

I am afraid that not many mothers know their children as a unique event. This is why they can think of a family in terms of number of mouths to feed, or college fees to pay, or even of what would be a "good number" of children to have. And our culture makes it very difficult for them to see this is any other way.

At one time I had a student from the Middle East who was making a study of the conception of the self, of "the person" in her country. She said to me, "If in my country you introduce a speaker, you say, this is the father of Ibrahim and Fatima." I was very much impressed and I told this story with much appreciation to an associate of mine who was working in a child development center. She was delighted with it. The next time I gave a talk, she was to introduce me, so she said, "I would like to introduce Mrs. Lee in the way she would like to be introduced. She is the mother of four children." She was so steeped in our cultural befogging of who-ness that she was unable to even hear what I said.

A mother has to be, I feel, very much aware of this point, particularly at this time when we gripe about dehumanization and keep attacking automation and industrialization. I think automation cannot depersonalize me, unless I allow it to. It has made and can make life very much richer for us, and instead of starting to attack it we should say, "render things to Caesar that are Caesar's and to God that are God's." Let industry talk about us as though we are numbers. We can be vital statistics when this is a needed short cut without losing individuality—so long as we are people in human situations, in the act of relatedness. I think this is where the woman, and particularly the mother, comes in. The mother, if she recognizes the who-ness of the child, is doing exactly this, is helping to generate and strengthen individuality that is as idiosyncratic as a signature.

One other aspect of our culture is relevant here. When we think of life, even when we are concerned with life itself, we seem to stop at the biological fact of life. This not only applies to the decision to have a child; it is an attitude toward a great variety of situations. For instance, a child is born with the wrong kind of blood and is in terrible danger. This news goes all over the country through television and radio. Blood is rushed to the child from another part of the country and the child lives. What happens to this child who may be the sixth child of an unemployed house painter living in a crowded slum? Does anybody ever think of what happens to this life? Which of the people who were so concerned with keeping this child from dying are now concerned with the span of life? There are societies where to save a man from dying means to take on a lifelong responsibility, a lifelong relationship.

The Greeks used to have two words for life: *zoe*, which refers to the either-alive-or-dead kind of life; and the word *bios*, from which we get the word biography—that is, the span of life. The mother must realize that she makes a decision for both of these: she makes a decision to bring a child into physical being; but whether she is aware of it or not, she also makes a decision for a bios. Does she know this? Has she, simultaneously, committed herself to see that this child is going to live a meaningful life? That, when he is aware of his situation, he will not say, as many of my students have said to me, "I am here, you can see me—yet I have never been born." The decision that a child is to be has to be recognized as a tremendously serious and responsible act. The mother has to know that she has made an unending commitment, an irretractable promise.

From now on I am going to be even more eclectic. I shall discuss a few of the points occurring in the literature directed to parents that give me particular worry.

First, I shall return to the advice to recognize difference, and relate it to the implicit suggestion to see the child as a member of a category. There was a time when mothers reading the work of people such as Gesell were worried to find that their four-month-old did not behave like Gesell's four-month-old. Now they are told not to worry, that each four-month-old proceeds at his own pace—within limits, of course. But they are still subtly encouraged to see him as a member of a category—not as *this* child, my Sue, but as a four-month-old; what they are told is not to worry if she deviates from the norm of the category. I consider this so destructive that I find it hard to forgive; and yes, I can speak this personally because it is *my* world, *my* people, who are being destroyed. I think that the new advice is no improvement over the old; and in addition it gives mothers the phony feeling that they recognize the uniqueness of the child.

To view in terms of category, whether as legitimately deviating from the norm or not, is a meager and a lazy substitute for knowing.

Take me, for instance—I am different than all of you. I have white hair, I have a Greek accent—I came to this country from Greece—I am an anthropologist. So, when you have listed all this, do you really know me? It is easy for you to list all the things that make me different, it is easy to categorize me professionally—but do you know *me?* And yet in our society quite often we fool ourselves by thinking that if we recognize differences, then we know.

Classification on the basis of difference is not even a category —it is a noncategory based on what is outside the being, the inner being, of the person. If a mother is going to help her child to be, she has to recognize what the child *is*, not what the child *is not*. What the child *is not* may, of course, come to be seen incidentally, though I think there are many societies in which what a child *is not* is a matter of complete indifference. The important thing is to recognize what the child *is*.

Recognizing and greeting the child as a *who*, as *this* child, is tremendously demanding. It is much more difficult than cooking and washing and lifting and picking up and cleaning house, and immeasurably more rewarding. It demands full commitment to the situation, with all one's senses and other capacities *there*, alive and straining and alert. For people who have learned to flinch from full engagement in experience, this is not easy; they have to fight and overcome strong resistance within themselves. Yet to do this, to my mind, means to choose life, existence, for the mother and the child. To seek the easy, to feel and perceive lazily, is for me a small death.

I will speak next about permissiveness. I know that by now to attack it is fashionable, in fact almost a bromide, but I want to attack it in my own way, for my own reasons. It has been attacked on the basis that children need limits, but to say that children need limits is for me too negative a statement of the issue. I would like to say that permissiveness where it exists or as it has existed is an evil and has done harm far beyond the fact that it does not give limits to the child.

Consider a one- or two-year-old infant. Can you imagine the miracle of this child learning language at a time when his brain presumably is at the beginning of his development, when his senses and his abilities to comprehend are so rudimentary? Yet he has to learn a language without a book, without direction, by simply listening, listening with all his senses. He has to find out for himself which part of the sentence "Come and get your apple" refers to the apple, which to the act, which to himself.

I know how difficult this is because I studied and recorded an Indian language from scratch, listening to the talk of the people. I would put down a couple of lines and I would look at them and wonder which was the verb, which was the noun, and what it meant. What did that ending to the verb refer to? Tense, or number, or something I never dreamed of? A baby has to do just this, and must learn to distinguish future from past, plural from singular, and so on. And he is not a trained linguist, nor a scholar trained in methodological analysis.

Now, after many years of language teaching, we have learned that the baby's way is the best way to learn a language. We pay people great amounts to give us a very intensive and special course in which just this situation is reproduced. Special institutions have developed centers for particular languages at great expense, drawing on great resources of knowledge, aided by electronic devices. The baby has to do all this for himself. He is flung into a world of confusion out of which he has to make his own order. And language is only one aspect of the culture he has to make his own. No anthropologist going out into the field after twenty years of schooling has a job as difficult as the one the baby has, and no anthropologist that I know has come out with such successful knowledge of a culture in all its details as a baby does.

A baby needs help in this staggering undertaking. In a so-called permissive setting he gets no help at all. He will have to discover values from such things as a gesture, or the expression in the mother's face, or the way she arranges the table—without any assistance. The baby needs help in taking on the rules of the culture, and also in taking on relatedness, his place in society, and his responsibility to society. The primitive people who managed to rear the most autonomous people I know are the Dakota Indians of this country; a hundred years ago, the parents, but particularly mothers, took on the job of carefully introducing a child step by step to culture, bit by bit to the values, then moving on and enabling him to choose and pass judgment on the basis of what had been clearly stated as the values of the society. Within this context, an individual engaged in unfiltered experience.

These people were not permissive, yet—or should I say "and therefore"—the people who grew this way were individuals who were strong. They were people who were autonomous and sure, not needing to test themselves or others all the time, not needing to give an account of themselves, justify themselves, or excuse themselves to themselves; at least this is what I get out of the autobiographies of Dakotas who were born about one hundred years ago. Within the cultural given, the child was encouraged to live his own body, live his own experience, piercingly, with support but no protective padding. So then, to my mind, one of the tasks of the mother who decides to bring a life into being is to teach the child to transact with the environment by presenting the environment clearly to the child—to present the cultural and social environment in its context of value, and on this firm floor, to stand by the child through the infinite exertion necessary for creative perception, for the development of personal style.

Another point about permissiveness that has not been nphasized is that permissiveness has meant for a number of people an encouragement to be spiritually lazy. It freed them from the need to be strongly involved. Involvement requires exertion, alertness, undeviating attention, and outgoing strength. Many people avoid becoming involved—it is much easier to be permissive.

I first discovered this fact from my students about ten years ago. I had a group of seniors who were discussing autonomy. They said, "Let's go around the table and have each of us tell at what point our parents allowed us to make our decisions as to when we would come home after our dates." They were all girls and the first one said, "When I was thirteen I came back whenever I wanted to." Six girls said something of the sort, and the last one added: "But I used to pretend that my mother told me to come home at twelve, because I wanted to show that she cared." The girls started discussing this and every one of them, at least fourteen girls, had felt that her mother did not care enough to tell them when to come home. I pursued this in a talk with mothers, and one woman, talking about her child, said, "When she comes to me and says, 'I want to do so and so, shall I do it?' I say to her, 'Do whatever you want, I don't care what you do.'" I said to this mother: "Listen to what you have said. Remember you said, 'I don't care.'" In these cases, permissiveness, as perceived by the daughters and as expressed by the mother, is the mandate for noninvolvement. This is what I call spiritual laziness.

My vision can be foggy, my hearing blurred, and I can still act permissively. If I am really concerned to help the child grow strong in personal discipline, my perception has to be sharp and attentive, so that I can distinguish the fine strivings of inquiry and thrust to whose growth I am committed. In the autobiographies of the Dakota, to which I referred above, this is what impresses me: the dialogue between the discipline-engendering adult and the searching child who is enabled to grow within himself the discipline he needs for the freedom to be.

My next point refers to what I said earlier about the mother who is ideally a person and not simply mother. This is also one thing that we must offer to our children, enabling them to have a *bios*, more than simply being alive. Whether we want it or not we are "mothers" for our children, and the question is: What as a mother do we offer to the child, and in what way do we enable the child to imitate the people in his society? The Dakota Indians have talked about that. . . . For those people the parents very clearly knew that they were mothers and they told their children to imitate them. Imitation for most of us means just copying, conformity; but this is not what the Dakotas asked of their children. First of all, the parents had to be worthy of imitation. Secondly, they made it even harder for themselves by starting with the child's ability to observe and enhancing, ramifying, refining, and strengthening this ability. The child, in imitating, first of all observed in incredible detail what was being done, what was being valued, and then followed—not merely reproducing, but using this new knowledge in creating their own lives. I must repeat that the parents saw to it that they were worthy of imitation.

I would like to bring up another point, which applies not only to mothers but to people in general—the point of "understanding." I want to criticize understanding, because I myself do not want to be understood. I want to be known, to be recognized, to generate joy or outrage or disgust; but I don't want to be understood. If I am, my very integrity is molested; it is disintegrated, probed, analyzed —all with the very best motives. The minute a person understands me, encounter is blocked, befogged by the theory that must underlie his diagnosis. Beyond that, I find in understanding something of condescension that is often a dimension of kindly attempts in our society. I don't want to be understood, and I don't want to understand *my* child. I want to be awed by the mystery of his existence, to be flooded and shaken over a timeless glimpse of human dignity.

In our society our job is to destroy mystery. Mystery is a challenge to solution; I feel uncomfortable until I explain it away. This is why I have to understand—so that I can grasp, so that I am in a position to manipulate. We leave it to our artists and poets to reach the mystery in immediacy, and leave it whole. Césaire says that Africans "wed" themselves to the mystery. That is what I want to do—to wed myself to inviolate being, to greet and respond. The very act of understanding carries with it the implication of belittlement. In this act, I insult the being of my child, and I cheat myself of the ineffable sense of miracle.

I want to bring up one last point, about another subject that has been talked about too much. And that is love. This is what I have been talking about. To know, and to want to know, in purity and immediacy, is to love. Love is not an easy thing; it is not just something that happens to me. Love is an act. I *choose* to love. Love is a strong, effortful response to the being of another, of my child. It demands exertion, it demands alertness, it demands that all of me be mobilized.

Yes, it is also comfortable, warmth-diffusing, and wonderful, but it is more than that. It is Césaire's "wedding"; it is an act of recognition, a kind of greeting to the dignity of the other. For me it is infinitely preferable to what goes under the name of equality, which I find minimal and an emergency ideal at best. If I am touched and shaken by the dignity of my child, the issue of equality becomes nonsense.

When love is knowing, it is not blind. I am afraid that many mothers try to retouch their children before they can bear to look at them; or they blur their vision and dull their hearing first. In this way, a mother doesn't have to recognize her daughter's small meannesses, her carelessness, her furtive cruelty, her cheating. And in the avoidance of recognition, the mother rejects her daughter and encourages her daughter to reject herself. To choose to know, to choose to love, is an act of commitment ultimately demanding all of the mother's self, and an act of response to the human dignity of her daughter. At this moment, the mother chooses "to be"—for her self and for her child.